ELIZABETH CADY STANTON
AND
WOMEN'S LIBERTY

MAKERS OF AMERICA

ELIZABETH CADY STANTON
AND
WOMEN'S LIBERTY

KATHRYN CULLEN-DUPONT

Facts On File
New York • Oxford

Elizabeth Cady Stanton and Women's Liberty

Facts On File, Inc.
460 Park Avenue South
New York NY 10016
USA

Facts On File Limited
Collins Street
Oxford OX4 1XJ
United Kingdom

Library of Congress Cataloging-in-Publication Data

Cullen-DuPont, Kathryn.
  Elizabeth Cady Stanton and women's liberty / Kathryn Cullen-DuPont
  p. cm. — (Makers of America)
  Includes bibliographical references and index.
  Summary: A biography of one of the first leaders of the women's rights movement, whose work led to the adoption of the nineteenth amendment—women's right to vote.
  ISBN 0-8160-2413-8
  1. Stanton, Elizabeth Cady, 1815-1902—Juvenile literature.
  2. Feminists—United States—Biography—Juvenile literature.
  [1. Stanton, Elizabeth Cady, 1815-1902. 2. Feminists. 3. Women's rights—History.] I. Title. II. Series: Makers of America (Facts On File, Inc.)
  HQ1413.S67C85   1992
  305.42'092—dc20
  [B]   91-21781

A British CIP catalogue record for this book is available from the British Library.

Facts On File books are available at special discounts when purchased in bulk quantities for businesses, associations, institutions or sales promotions. Please contact our Special Sales Department in New York at 212/683-2244 (dial 800/322- 8755 except in NY, AK, or HI) or in Oxford at 865/728399.

Text design by Ron Monteleone
Jacket design by Ron Monteleone
Composition by Facts On File, Inc.
Manufactured by R. R. Donnelly & Sons
Printed in the United States of America

10 9 8 7 6 5 4 3 2 1

This book is printed on acid-free paper.

For my son, Jesse Cullen-DuPont

CONTENTS

ELIZABETH CADY STANTON
AND
WOMEN'S LIBERTY

1

THE BRINK OF A PRECIPICE: 1840

May 10, 1840 was a Friday, an allegedly unlucky day to enter the state of matrimony. But Elizabeth Cady refused to worry. The day before, she'd finally decided to marry Henry Stanton; she would have married him that same afternoon, an uncontroversial Thursday, but Mr. Stanton's journey to her side via the North River (as the Hudson was then called) had been slowed by a sandbar.

His courtship of her had earlier faced its own impediments: he was a well-known abolitionist, that is, a person committed to working for an end to slavery and the granting of U.S. citizenship to black people in America. Many people held antislavery views that were more limited than the views held by abolitionists; for example, while some antislavery people felt that slavery was morally wrong, they nevertheless made no claims for the equality of black and white human beings and offered colonization—the deportation of black men and women to Africa or other destinations—as a way to rid the United States of slavery. Henry B. Stanton, then, as an abolitionist, belonged to the most radical segment of the antislavery movement. He was known for his brave silencing of hostile mobs, and Elizabeth thought him a hero. Her conservative father, Judge Daniel Cady, did not. Moreover, Henry Stanton was penniless. When Elizabeth first became betrothed to him, Judge Cady and other members of the Cady family insisted that she break her engagement. She did, but she would not stop corresponding with the man she loved. Henry Stanton had, Elizabeth thought, "one of the most eloquent pens of this generation." By letter alone, he was able to convince her of a future "as bright and beautiful as Spring." Then he wrote that he was going to Europe for several months as a delegate to the

World Anti-Slavery Convention. Elizabeth despaired. As she later recalled, she "did not wish the ocean to roll between us." Asked once more if she'd like to marry, Elizabeth Cady said "yes." She and Henry would elope.

Elizabeth didn't want her parents to suspect, so she didn't pack any clothing. She spoke only with her family's minister. Then, when Henry sent word that he had finally arrived in Johnstown, New York, Elizabeth donned "a simple white evening dress" and met him at the town's Presbyterian church.

The Reverend Hugh Marie had agreed to marry the couple in secrecy, but he had not agreed to Friday nuptials. Now he was begging them to wait. Tomorrow would be Saturday, he said, and much luckier. Elizabeth laughed. Henry Stanton was at her side, and a new life of love and freedom was about to begin. Friday's luck? She brushed that aside. Instead, she raised an objection of her own: to the marriage vow binding her "to love, honor and obey" her husband. "I obstinately refused," she later recalled in her autobiography, "to obey one with whom I supposed I was entering into an equal relation."

This was a shocking innovation in 1840. At the time, a man received control of a woman's body upon marriage: Once wed, a woman could not refuse her husband's sexual advances. The rare omission of "obey" from a bride's vows meant that she intended to grant or withhold consent according to her own desires. Henry Stanton, attending a wedding the year before, had heard another bride so refuse to "obey." Now he supported his own bride's wishes. The Reverend Marie, however, was very upset, and it was only at the end of a lengthy argument that he finally agreed to a Friday wedding with modified vows. Then, all obstacles to their union overcome, Elizabeth Cady and Henry B. Stanton were married.

If her sisters knew in advance of the elopement, or were present in the church, Elizabeth was careful to leave no evidence of it. Afterward, however, one of her younger sisters— Margaret, the most cherished playmate of Elizabeth's girlhood—accompanied the runaway couple to New York City. And one of Elizabeth's elder sisters, Harriet, rushed from her Manhattan home to the South Street seaport with her husband, Daniel Eaton. They arrived in time to board the *Montreal* and congratulate the newlyweds.

To Harriet's and Daniel's surprise, Elizabeth—usually confident once she'd made a decision—seemed overwhelmed by the enormity of this latest step. Certainly, she was finding it hard to say good-bye to her sisters and brother-in-law. And she knew that her parents, upon learning the news, might disown her. Judge Cady had once written to a relative on this very subject. Many fathers at the time expected, as Judge Cady put it, to see a daughter "settled in life agreeable to his [her father's] wishes." In the event a daughter "gay-giddy and ungrateful . . . [should] choose a husband whom he [her father] disliked," the judge thought it necessary for her father to "pray that God forgive her and make that marriage a prosperous one." But so long as this spiritual obligation was satisfied, Judge Cady wrote, the "cruelly disappointed" father could say of his daughter, "My feelings and my honor may not permit me to take her to my arms."

Daniel Eaton thought he should try to cheer his suddenly dispirited sister-in-law. When he'd first begun to court Harriet, Elizabeth had been a young girl, eager to engage him in repeated games of "tag." Now he gave chase and said she'd go "tagged to Europe." Elizabeth ran around the deck of the *Montreal*, trying hard to win. But, she later recalled, "as I was compelled, under the circumstances, to conduct the pursuit with some degree of decorum, and he had the advantage of height, long limbs, and freedom from skirts, I really stood no chance whatever." Nonetheless, " . . . the chase kept us all laughing, [and] it helped to soften the bitterness of parting." Elizabeth was smiling as the ship pulled away from the pier.

The *Montreal* was a 543-ton packet ship, built in 1833 to carry mail, passengers, and cargo across the Atlantic. Like all such sailing ships, it had three tall masts, each made from the trunk of a single white pine, and full, square sails. Steamships had begun to cross the Atlantic only two years before. With looks that a *New York Herald* reporter described as "long, low [and] piratical," these newer ships could sometimes make the trip to London in 13 days. The more traditional *Montreal*, in contrast, would be at sea for 18 days.

Elizabeth Cady had always been a person of naturally high spirits. Elizabeth Cady Stanton, as she now decided to call herself, remained so. She couldn't be still and quiet for 18 days. Like many a happy bride, she spent hours with her new husband. But she also found time to explore the ship. Before long, she became friendly with the captain, whom she considered "a jolly fellow," and with many of the crew members and other passengers. Not all of her sailing companions, however, were charmed by her youthful buoyancy. Among her sharpest critics was James G. Birney.

James Gillespie Birney was born in Kentucky on February 4, 1792, to slaveholding parents. His mother died when he was only three years old, and his paternal aunt, Mrs. Boyle, joined the family to care for her brother's children. Mrs. Boyle despised slavery and always paid any slave who helped her in the Birney home. Her nephew grew to despise the institution as well. Upon his graduation from Princeton in 1810 and completion of law studies, he was elected first, in 1814, to the town council of Danville, Kentucky, and then, in 1816, to the lower house of Kentucky's state assembly. It was the beginning of a career devoted to ending slavery. By the time he sailed to London and the World Anti-Slavery Convention, he had been elected the Liberty party's antislavery candidate for president of the United States.

As Henry Stanton and Birney were both members of the National Anti-Slavery Society, Elizabeth and her husband spent much of their time in Birney's company. It took Cady Stanton only a few days to decide that the presidential candidate "was a polished gentleman of the old school," with rather stuffy ideas about women. Birney just as quickly formed an opinion of his associate's young wife. Elizabeth Cady Stanton, he made clear, "needed considerable toning down before reaching England."

Cady Stanton did not display the deference that was expected of wives toward their husbands in the early 19th century. Birney wanted this changed.

"I heard you call your husband 'Henry' in the presence of strangers, which is not permissible in polite society," he told Cady Stanton one day. "You should always say 'Mr. Stanton.'"

"Mr. Stanton," upon learning of this rebuke, reassured his wife: Their marriage was their own, and not open to adjustment by Mr. Birney.

The reprimands continued. Cady Stanton had seen most of the ship, but her long skirts made it unsafe for her to climb the hemp ropes and ladders that led to the top of the ship's mast. One day, members of the crew hoisted her up on a chair rigged to ropes and a pulley. To her delight, a true sailor's view of the Atlantic was hers at last.

But back on deck she again faced Birney. "You went to the masthead in a chair, which I think very unladylike," he said in an accusing tone.

His criticisms increased. Finally, Cady Stanton laughingly replied, "Bless me! What a catalog in one day! I fear my mentor will despair of my ultimate perfection."

James Birney did not laugh in return. "I should have more hope if you seemed to feel my rebukes more deeply," he said, "but you evidently think them of too little consequence to be much disturbed by them."

He was right. She was more amused than disturbed by his comments aboard the *Montreal*. Growing up, she'd fought against attitudes such as Birney's, and won. She'd fought for, and received, the best possible education available to a young woman in America. She'd studied Greek and math, winning prizes the male students wanted for themselves. On horseback, she could jump any fence without fear. And so, aboard the *Montreal*, Elizabeth Cady Stanton confidently ignored Birney's ideas about women. She had no idea that soon, in London, she'd be "much disturbed by them" indeed.

She did have one immediate concern: her lack of specific knowledge about the abolitionist movement. In principle, she'd long taken an antislavery position, and she knew of the movement's most famous heroes and heroines. Now married to one of those very heroes, she was about to attend the World Anti-Slavery Convention at his side. Once there, Cady Stanton would meet the people she'd "worshiped from afar": the world's most liberal and progressive thinkers, the "teachers and leaders of men." She was thrilled. She was also determined to learn all she could about the antislavery movement. And on this subject Birney found his instructions welcome.

From the materials Henry Stanton and James Birney provided, Cady Stanton learned that abolitionists were deeply divided. Just recently, they'd split into two separate factions, generally known as "Garrisonians" and "anti-Garrisonians." The Garrisonians permitted women to join their societies and to become speakers and officers. The anti-Garrisonians thought the presence of women an "insane innovation," and refused them admission. This was not the only divisive issue.

William Lloyd Garrison, the charismatic leader of the Garrisonians, was considered too extreme by many abolitionists. Some of these, like Henry Stanton, supported women's rights but joined the less radical anti-Garrisonians nonetheless. And not all abolitionist women joined the more radical faction. Refused admission to the male anti-Garrisonian societies, these women decided to form Female Anti-Slavery Societies. By the time the ship neared the southern coast of England, Cady Stanton had learned enough to make a decision. She—unlike her husband and Birney—was a Garrisonian sympathizer.

Henry, Elizabeth, and their companions finally landed at Torquay, a lovely resort on England's Devonshire coast 26 miles south of Exeter. It was now June, and their first day in England seemed "like a journey in fairyland" to Cady Stanton. As four horses pulled the carriage toward Exeter, she found herself surrounded by gardens more beautiful than any she'd ever seen. Every tree, every shrub, had flowers; and when, in the early evening, they came upon Exeter Cathedral, they heard its choir practicing.

Exeter Cathedral is as beautiful now as it was then. All of England's other cathedrals have central towers. Exeter Cathedral has one tower on each side and, inside, a high vault, that is, an arched masonry ceiling, that seems simply to soar. The Americans found its beauty compelling. As Elizabeth described, "the deep tones of the organ reverberating through the arched roof, . . . the sound of human voices . . . trying to fill the vast space above . . . [and] the solemnity of the surroundings roused all our religious emotions and thrilled every nerve in our being." Although they needed to be in London as quickly as possible, all were "moved by the same impulse to linger . . . [and] sat down."

As she sat, Cady Stanton's feet would probably have rested on one of the many inscribed slabs that form large parts of the cathedral floor. Such slabs, like the tablets and plaques affixed to the walls, commemorate the dead who lie buried within the great cathedral. "Here lye the remains," she might have read on one black stone, "of Mary, the beloved wife of Stephen Weston, Esq. and daughter of John Gibbs, Esq. She departed this life the 4th day of July, 1739 in the 30th year of her age." Another plaque was "Sacred to the memory of Susannah, wife of Joseph Bealey M.D. . . . The amiable qualities of her heart

Exeter Cathedral (from engraving drawn by R. Garland and engraved by B. Winkles, 1837)

and an excellent and cultivated understanding insured . . . the esteem and admiration of all who knew her . . . Also in the same grave lieth her only child . . . aged 18 months." Before finally leaving the cathedral, Cady Stanton might have read tributes reaching back through many centuries.

The travelers reached London, 200 miles east of Exeter, after a long, exhausting carriage ride. Now it was not the sound of church music that predominated, but the sound of human voices. One contemporary, the author Henry Mayhew, described his city's background noise as "the Babel"—and with good reason: Everywhere one turned in 19th century London, there seemed to be a person selling something. Women and girls, known as costermongers, carried baskets of chestnuts, cherries, oranges, or pears, all for sale to hungry passersby. On one corner, an Irish peddler might shout, "fine ating apples!" On another, a man might offer carefully collected birds' nests, the eggs still inside. On a typical day, Mayhew wrote, "[t]he tumult of the thousand different cries . . . is almost bewildering. 'So-old again,' roars one. 'Chestnuts all 'ot, a penny a score,' bawls another . . . 'Twopence a pound grapes.'" And in the midst of all this, he recorded, would sit "the girl with her basket of walnuts [who] lifts her brown-stained fingers to her mouth, as she screams, 'Fine warnuts! sixteen a penny, fine war-r-nuts!'"

Elizabeth and Henry made their way through the crowded streets, passing world-renowned buildings and parks. Over the next few weeks, Cady Stanton would explore many of them: Regent's Park with its promenade and Zoological Gardens (residence at the time to giraffes, leopards, tigers, zebras, and what one astonished American described as "the largest elephant and rhinoceros in Europe"); Westminster Abbey with its beloved Poets' Corner; St. James's Palace and the Houses of Parliament; the British Museum, the India Museum, and others; the spectacularly domed St. Paul's Cathedral; and the pedestrians' tunnel beneath the Thames River, then in the midst of excavation. Now, though, she and Henry were tired. They made their way directly to their lodgings.

At No. 6 Queen Street the couple found a small chamber with a view of the original Blackfriar's Bridge, completed in 1769. More important to Cady Stanton, they also found female delegates to the World Anti-Slavery Convention. Abby Southwick,

The Thames Tunnel (from engraving)

Emily Winslow, and another newly married woman, Ann Green Phillips, came as delegates of Boston's American Female Anti-Slavery Society. Another group of women came from Philadelphia: Mary Grew, whose father, the Reverend Henry Grew, was a delegate as well; Elizabeth Neall, the granddaughter of Warner Muffin, who would be described at the convention as "the first man who liberated his slaves unconditionally"; Sarah Pugh and Abby Kimber, both Quakers; and the famous Lucretia Mott.

Lucretia Coffin Mott was born 47 years earlier in Nantucket, Massachusetts, the second of seven children in a Quaker family. Her father, Thomas Coffin, was a sea captain. Her mother, Anna Folger Coffin, managed her family alone for many months each year. Many other Nantucket women did the same, and this largely female culture inspired the young girl. "I grew up so thoroughly imbued with women's rights," she later said, "that it was the most important question of my life from a very early day." She became a teacher and was outraged to discover that female teachers were paid less than half the salary paid to male teachers. Despite her anger, she fell in love with one of these male colleagues. Lucretia Coffin and James Mott were married on April 10, 1811. They made their home in Philadelphia. There, they buried one child, their second, and raised their five other children.

The Motts' marriage was a wonderfully close and loving one, and the beliefs they came to hold were acted upon both within and without their home. James Mott had left teaching and entered the lucrative cotton trade. After listening to a famous minister speak against slavery, and particularly against the use of products produced by enslaved people, Lucretia and James examined their consciences. From that day forward, Lucretia allowed neither cotton nor slave-grown sugar, nor any other such product, in her home. Five years later, James left the cotton trade and turned to Northern wool.

In 1818, Lucretia Mott was herself recorded as a Quaker minister. She began to speak against slavery, first in her own meetinghouse, and later, in other public places. In 1833, she attended the founding convention of the American Anti-Slavery Society, only to find that women were not welcome. Undeterred, she helped in that same year to found the Philadelphia Female Anti-Slavery Society. By 1837, there were many other female antislavery societies, and Mott helped organize the Anti-Slavery Convention of American Women. The women met again in 1838. This infuriated anti-abolitionists, as the opponents of the antislavery movement were called. Two days after the women spoke at Pennsylvania Hall, an anti-abolitionist mob burned it down. Then they marched toward the Mott home. Lucretia Mott waited there for them, determined not to budge.

Fortunately, Lucretia Mott, her family, and her home were spared. She was now in London, indisputably the most celebrated of American abolitionist women. And Cady Stanton, who had "often longed to meet some woman who had sufficient confidence in herself to frame and hold an opinion in the face of opposition, a woman . . . to whom I could talk freely," found herself seated beside Lucretia Mott at dinner.

Birney was also staying at No. 6 Queen Street, and he was dismayed by the number of active, independent women joining him for dinner. When other male delegates also joined the group, a lively discussion of "the woman question" began. "I found myself in full accord with the other ladies," Cady Stanton remembered, "combating most of the gentlemen at the table . . . In spite of constant gentle nudgings from my husband under the table, and frowns from Mr. Birney opposite, the tantalizing tone of the conversation was too much for me to maintain silence. Calmly and skillfully Mrs. Mott parried all their attacks, now by her quiet humor turning the laugh on them, and then by her earnestness and dignity silencing their ridicule and sneers. I shall never forget the look of recognition she gave me when she saw by my remarks that I fully comprehended the problem of woman's rights and wrongs. How beautiful she looked to me that day."

Within days, Birney found other lodgings. Lucretia Mott stayed and wrote in her diary, "Elizabeth Stanton growing daily in our affections."

Cady Stanton, for her part, "sought every opportunity to be at her [Lucretia Mott's] side." She found their conversations inspiring. "It seemed to me like meeting a being from some higher planet," Elizabeth explained, "to find a woman who dared question the opinions of Popes, Kings, Synods, [and] Parliaments, . . . recognizing no higher authority than the judgment of a pure-minded, educated woman. When I first heard from the lips of Lucretia Mott that I had the same right to think for myself that [religious leaders] Luther, Calvin, and John Knox had, and the same right to be guided by my own convictions . . . I felt at once a new-born sense of dignity and freedom."

Unfortunately, her newborn senses were quickly assaulted. The World Anti-Slavery Convention took place in Freemason's Hall, London, and began on June 12, 1840. Its first act was to refuse admission to the female delegates.

Wendell Phillips was the son of Boston's first mayor and a leader among Garrisonian abolitionists. His wife, Ann Green Phillips, was among the women told to leave. Phillips angrily leaped up to defend her and the other female delegates. "Massachusetts," he said of his and Ann's home state, "has for several years acted on the principle of admitting women to an equal seat with men, in the deliberative bodies of anti-slavery societies . . . we do not think it just or equitable . . . that, after the trouble, the sacrifice, the self-devotion of a part of those who leave their families . . . and occupations . . . to come three thousand miles to attend this World's Convention, they should be refused a place in its deliberations."

Mary Grew's father disagreed. As his daughter stood before him, the Reverend Henry Grew declared: "The reception of women as part of this Convention would, in the view of many, be not only a violation of the customs of England, but of the ordinance of Almighty God."

The women were stunned; so were some of the men. "You will take away the rights of one-half of creation?" asked one, Mr. Ashurst, in disbelief. Remarkably, he was not referring to slavery. Suddenly, women had become the subject of the World Anti-Slavery Convention.

Not one woman was allowed to take the floor to speak for herself. Instead, male delegates were given turns to say just what they thought about women. Little of it was good. Most argued that women, because of their "delicacy," must be "protected," that is, segregated and kept from involvement in public life. Others described women as inferior people with "shrinking natures," unfit for life outside the home.

Many, echoing the Reverend Grew, invoked religious sanctions to rationalize their prejudices. The Reverend A. Harvey, of Glasgow, Scotland, was one. "If I were to give a vote in favor of females," he said, "sitting and deliberating in such an assembly as this . . . I should be acting in opposition to the plain teaching of the Word of God."

Elizabeth Cady Stanton felt "humiliated and chagrined." She knew that Lucretia Mott was herself a minister, and that all her female companions were "remarkable women, speakers and leaders." She was also shocked that "abolitionists, who felt so keenly the wrongs of the slave, should be so oblivious to the equal wrongs of their own mothers, wives, and sisters, when, according to the common law, both classes occupied a similar legal status."

But not all male delegates were oblivious. Wendell Phillips was continuing to fight for the women. He'd listened to all the prejudiced statements, and now he answered. "In America we listen to no such arguments. If we had done so," he insisted, "we had never been here as Abolitionists. It is the custom there not to admit colored men into respectable society, and we have been told again and again that we are outraging the decencies of humanity when we permit colored men to sit by our side. When we have submitted to brick-bats, and the tar tub and feathers in America, rather than yield to the custom prevalent there of not admitting colored brethren into our friendship, shall we yield to parallel custom of prejudice against women . . . ?"

Henry Stanton, acting as secretary of the convention, made a speech in favor of admitting the women. Sarah Pugh composed a written protest on behalf of herself and her silenced friends. William Lloyd Garrison, not yet arrived in London but worried about the reception the female delegates might be receiving, wrote to his wife, "With a young woman [Queen Victoria] placed on the throne of Great Britain, will the philanthropists of that country presume to object to the female delegates from the United States, as members of the Convention, on the ground of their sex?"

As it happened, the queen's bravery was well noted during this week. She'd been but a young woman when she'd ascended the throne in 1837. Described by the English writer Thomas Carlyle as a "nice sonsy [sweet] little lassie; blue eyes, light hair, fine white skin; of extremely small stature," Queen Victoria was now expecting her first child. On June 10th, 1840, just two days before the World Anti-Slavery Convention opened, a man named Edward Oxford tried to assassinate the pregnant woman. As Mary Grew recorded in her diary, " . . .

the Queen had been twice shot at, while riding . . . Her majesty received no injury, and immediately stood up in her carriage, to show her people, who were fast gathering around her, that she was unhurt. She was not much alarmed, and continued her ride, for three quarters of an hour, escorted by crowds of gentlemen on horseback, who thronged around her carriage, eager to protect the person of their youthful sovereign."

Dr. Bowring, a male delegate from America, remarked upon the queen, hoping respect for her might be extended to all members of the sex: "In this country sovereign rule is placed in the hands of a female . . . [while] we are associated with a body of Christians (Quakers) who have given to their women a great, honorable, and religious prominence."

Tongue-tied attempts to dismiss the queen's significance followed. "I . . . commend to the consideration of our American female friends who are so deeply interested in the subject," said one American, the Reverend Eben Galusha, "the example of your noble Queen, who by sanctioning her consort, His Royal Highness Prince Albert, in taking the chair on an occasion not dissimilar to this, showed her sense of propriety by putting her Head foremost in an assembly of gentlemen. I have no objection to woman's being the neck to turn the head aright," he explained, "but do not wish to see her assume the place of the head."

The argument continued and grew loud. Most of the clergy continued to oppose the admission of women, and some of them started waving their Bibles overhead for emphasis. George Bradburn was no member of the clergy, but a Massachusetts state legislator and tireless antislavery worker. He was also six feet tall, muscular, and in possession of what Elizabeth Cady Stanton called a "voice of thunder." Angry to see Bibles so used, he stood. "Prove to me, gentlemen," he exclaimed, "that your Bible sanctions the slavery of woman—the complete subjugation of one-half of the race to the other—and I should feel that the best work I could do for humanity would be to make a grand bonfire of every Bible in the Universe!"

But this was a minority viewpoint. By the end of the day it was clear that most of the men were against the women. It was clear, too, that some of these "leaders and teachers of men," as Cady Stanton had previously termed them, didn't even think women's rights had been worth the discussion.

"Shall we be divided on this *paltry question,*" an impatient Reverend Stout said in dismissal, "and suffer the whole tide of benevolence to be stopped by *a straw?* No!" he insisted. "You talk of being men, then be men! Consider what is worthy of your attention!"

And so, the male delegates voted. Women were disallowed as delegates and removed to seats behind a curtain. They would be able to hear the proceedings, but they would not be permitted to see them or to speak.

As Phillips watched his wife and her colleagues being led away, he made what he hoped was a healing statement. "There is no unpleasant feeling in our mind," he said. "I have no doubt that women will sit with as much interest behind the bar . . . "

William Lloyd Garrison, arriving after the vote, thought otherwise. "After battling so many long years for the liberties of African slaves," declared this ardent champion of the abolitionist cause, "I can take no part in a convention that strikes down the most sacred rights of all women." He joined the women behind their curtain where, as Elizabeth Cady Stanton described, "after coming three thousand miles to speak on the subject nearest his heart, he nobly shared the enforced silence of the rejected delegates."

Cady Stanton couldn't believe that Phillips and other sympathetic men failed to understand the matter as Garrison did. "Would there have been no unpleasant feelings," she wrote, immediately thinking of two African-American males central to the abolitionist movement, " . . . had Frederick Douglass and Robert Purvis been refused their seats in a convention of reformers under similar circumstances? and, had *they* listened one entire day to debates on their peculiar fitness for plantation life, and unfitness for the forum and public assemblies, and been rejected as delegates on the ground of color, could Wendell Phillips have so far mistaken their real feelings, and been so insensible to the insults offered them, as to have told a Convention of men who had just trampled on their most sacred rights, that 'they would no doubt sit with as much interest behind the bar, as in the Convention?'"

It was not Phillips' but the Reverend Dr. Morrison's assessment that the women shared. "I believe," he said, "that we are treading on the brink of a precipice."

Later that night, Lucretia Mott and Elizabeth Cady Stanton were walking through the London streets. Throughout the day, they'd heard woman described as a sheltered, dainty, timid creature in need of a protection that she mustn't give up. Yet a simple stroll down Great Queen Street was enough to make one wonder: What protection did men really think women had? Poor women continued down the street with their baskets of fruit, even

The Coster Girl (from Henry Mayhew's *London Labour and the London Poor*)

as darkness settled. Young girls still peddled their flowers. Educated, self-confident women had been refused a voice. Could their less fortunate sisters even *hope* to speak?

Throughout the day, women delegates had murmured back and forth. Women needed more than memorial plaques in cathedrals, more than permission to sell wares on street corners, more than segregated seating away from the world's affairs. Behind the curtain, women had agreed. "It is about time," they'd whispered, "some demand was made for new liberties for women."

Before retiring for the night, Lucretia Mott and Elizabeth Cady Stanton decided to make that demand. Once back in America, they'd hold a convention of their own: "A woman's convention."

The brink of a precipice had indeed been reached.

2

ELIZABETH CADY: 1815–29

It was 1814, and the War of 1812 with Great Britain was coming to a close. America had entered the war in response to Britain's impressment, or kidnapping, of American sailors, who were then forced to help Britain in its war against France. As the United States' strategy included trying to conquer Canada, which was then under British rule, many important battles had been fought in the western frontiers of New York State and on its waterways.

Now the British government was interested in beginning peace talks, and President Madison's team of negotiators was on its way to Europe. Before the year was out, the Treaty of Ghent would be signed. America would enter a peacetime described in one Boston newspaper as the "Era of Good Feelings." The Erie Canal would be built, and New York's waterways—of such consequence during the war—would increase in national importance.

It was in this year, 1814, and in this influential state, New York, that Judge Daniel Cady was elected to the United States Congress. Following "the excitement of a political campaign," Judge Cady's wife, Margaret Livingston Cady, became pregnant. She gave birth to a daughter who later half-jokingly claimed that her mother's political interests must "have had an influence on my prenatal life." This child, born November 12, 1815, was the eighth child and fourth daughter born to Judge Daniel and Margaret Livingston Cady. Her name was Elizabeth Cady.

At the time of Elizabeth's birth, this large family lived in a two-story wooden house at Johnstown, New York, along with several servants. Johnstown is situated in the Mohawk Valley, which was once home to Hiawatha and the Iroquois Confederacy. It was founded by Britain's Sir William Johnson in 1762, two years after he led a troop of Native Americans into battle against the French in Montreal and several years after his marriage to Molly Brant, sister of the famous Mohawk chief Joseph Brant. By 1815, this town was home to 1,000 people.

Margaret Cady loved living in Johnstown. Her husband did not. Daniel Cady was a very wealthy man, and he wanted to move his family to a large country estate. It was obvious, he said, that their present home was too small. Margaret Cady agreed with him about the size of the house. Nevertheless, she refused to leave Johnstown. A member of one of New York's oldest Dutch families and daughter of James Livingston, who had served under George Washington in the American Revolution, Margaret Cady was tall, independent, gregarious—and, as her daughter would later say, "queenly." She enjoyed the easy sociability of town life and the opportunities it offered for involvement in church or community affairs. Eventually, Judge Cady gave up his demand for a country estate. Instead, he had the white frame house torn down and a large, brick mansion built on the same site.

And so, throughout Elizabeth's childhood, Margaret Cady continued to enjoy Johnstown. Its streets and sidewalks were laid out in an orderly fashion: Large cobblestones paved the streets, and small cobblestones paved the sidewalks. Poplar trees lined the road, providing summer shade to farmers in their wagons. The Cayadutta River wound its picturesque way through and then around the northern part of town. Children came there to wade. The river also provided power for the factories that had recently been built in town. The school and church were both painted white; among the largest buildings in Johnstown, they'd later be equaled in size by the new Cady home.

Elizabeth quickly became a sturdy, plump little girl. She had brown hair, fair pink skin, and blue eyes that were always described as "laughing." She eagerly joined the other children outdoors. Although winters in northern New York were sometimes as cold as 20° below, she played in the snow whenever she could. In summer's heat, she sometimes squeezed through the barred windows of her nursery and sat down on the slightly sloped roof, "enjoying the moon and stars" and the muffled sounds of the street.

Margaret Livingston Cady (Courtesy of Vassar College Library)

She found much to enjoy indoors as well. Elizabeth's favorite rooms in her first home were the garret and cellar. As in other early 19th-century houses, these rooms were used to store almost a year's necessities. The garret, at the top of the house, contained barrels of nuts and other baking stuffs. Cakes of maple sugar were stored there (for nibbling, the children thought), and the family's dried herbs were spread out or hung in fragrant bunches. Everything needed to clothe a family was stored there as well. Packages of fabric—calico, cotton, flannel, and silk—were piled alongside old spinning wheels. Best of all was the small window, a "scuttle hole," from which one got a view of the entire countryside.

The cellar was completely dark unless candles were lit. At the end of autumn, this cool space was filled with food for the coming winter: barrels of fruits and vegetables, large pieces of salted meat, jugs of cider, and a supply of butter. Elizabeth and the other Cady children liked this room for games such as blind man's bluff and hide-and-seek.

As a child, Elizabeth also participated in her town's public celebrations. Independence Day was acknowledged then with oration as well as gunpowder. People waited through the night of July 3rd for midnight to arrive, and then lit cannons and bonfires. Sounds of bells, firecrackers, and artillery fire greeted the "dawn's early light" and continued throughout the morning. Later, citizens and soldiers paraded through the town, and a respected member of the community delivered a speech. Then, the highlight: a reading aloud of the Declaration of Independence. When evening and hunger finally arrived, the people of Johnstown gathered on the lawn of their courthouse for a picnic dinner.

Another civic event, Training Day, was held in September. On that day, the county militia presented itself for review. The troops marched in unison around the oval racetrack while the townspeople cheered and waved. Farmers came, too, with sweets, pies, and the first of their harvests in wagons. Elizabeth Cady enjoyed Training Day—especially, she said later, for its gingerbread and molasses candy.

Daniel Cady was a prominent member of this community. He'd served in the New York state legislature in Albany, just 40 miles away, from 1808 until 1814. His career in the United States Congress lasted two years, until 1816. He then served as a circuit court judge and, later, as an associate justice of New York's Supreme Court. Judge Cady's reputation, and the appeal of Johnstown itself, drew many bright young law students to work in his office.

All these students were male, and Judge Cady included them as much as possible in family life. Two of his own sons, both named Daniel, had died before Elizabeth was born—one had been eight years old, the other, four months. Another son, James, had died in 1809, no older than 14 months. After these losses, Judge Cady especially treasured his surviving son, Eleazar, and his own role as mentor to his young clerks. He was thoroughly delighted, later on, when four of them joined his family as sons-in-law.

Nonetheless, Judge and Margaret Cady wished desperately for another son of their own. Their first-born, a daughter named Harriet, had died in 1810, when she'd been only seven or eight years old. By the time of Elizabeth's birth, then, only four of the Cady's eight children survived: their three daughters, Tryphena, Harriet Eliza, and Elizabeth; and their son, Eleazar. The birth of another child, Margaret, nicknamed Little Madge, increased the number of Cady children to five. But, to Judge and Margaret Cady's regret, Eleazar was still the only living son.

In 1819, when Elizabeth was four years old, Margaret Cady gave birth for the 10th time. Elizabeth was excited and curious, and she couldn't wait to visit the baby. Finally, the nurse took her in "to see the little stranger." To her surprise and dismay, she heard her mother's friends say, one after another: "What a pity it is she's a girl!" That pitied girl was named Catherine Henry Cady. Elizabeth Cady felt an instant compassion for her baby sister. She was so struck by the incident, and so confused, that it became her earliest memory. "I did not understand at that time that girls were considered an inferior order of beings," she later wrote.

All the Cady daughters were taught reading and writing at what was called a "dame school"—a school run by a woman in her home. Marie Yost, an unmarried woman in Johnstown, had run such a school for the benefit of three generations of girls. She was friendly, cheerful, and capable. Under her tutelage, Elizabeth soon mastered the lessons in *Murray's Spelling Book*, a reader in use at the time. She mastered her lessons in acute discomfort, though. Girls normally wore skirts every day, and the Cady sisters were no exception. They went to school in red stockings, heavy, red flannel dresses with starched ruffles at the throats, and black aprons. (On Sundays, they were allowed white aprons.) Whenever Elizabeth complained that the ruffle scratched her skin, she was scolded. If she dared to touch it, to try to loosen it, her hand was slapped and the ruffled collar made tighter.

She disliked her restrictive clothing. Indeed, she disliked restriction of any kind. She was particularly absorbed in her thoughts one day, and her nurse, Mary Dunn, noticed. Years later, the ensuing conversation was recounted in Elizabeth Cady Stanton's autobiography.

"Child," Mary Dunn asked, "what are you thinking about? Are you planning some new form of mischief?"

"No, Mary," Elizabeth replied, "I was wondering why it was that everything we like to do is a sin, and that everything we dislike is commanded by God or someone on earth. I am so tired," she continued, "of that everlasting no! no! no! At school, at home, everywhere it is *no!* Even at church all the commandments begin 'Thou shalt not.' I suppose God will say 'no' to all we like in the next world, just as you do here."

Mary Dunn was shocked and appalled. But Elizabeth's sister Margaret was inspired. Though two years younger than Elizabeth, she was taller and, Elizabeth thought, "stronger . . . and more fearless and self-reliant." Margaret came to Elizabeth several days later.

"I tell you what to do," she said. "Hereafter let us act as we choose, without asking."

Now Elizabeth was shocked. "Then we shall be punished."

"Suppose we are," Margaret responded, "we shall have had our fun at any rate, and that is better than to mind the everlasting 'no' and not have any fun at all."

Elizabeth agreed. The two sisters defied both parental authority and the weight of their skirts. They explored the forest. They waded into the Cayadutta and gathered pebbles from its bottom. And once, miscalculating their strength and ability, they tried to ferry their girlfriends across the mill pond on a raft. Instead, they took their friends right over the dam and into the river itself! They were happy with self-government, though, and eventually congratulated themselves for having "risen above our infantile fear of punishment."

Young Elizabeth may not have been impressed by parental or divine authority. She grew ever more impressed, however, by the authority of laws passed in a democracy. The daughters of the hotel keeper and the local sheriff were Elizabeth's good friends. Each year during "court week," she visited the jailhouse with the sheriff's daughter. The two girls brought cakes to the prisoners and asked about their alleged crimes and possible punishments. Then they accompanied the hotel keeper's daughter to the dining room. Since it was filled with judges and lawyers, they overheard conversations about the pending court cases. Elizabeth realized that the prisoners might really stay in jail and that some might even be hanged.

Finally, still fascinated, the children attended court: Elizabeth, especially, wanted to hear the arguments and verdicts for herself.

When court was not in session, Elizabeth frequented her father's office. There, she had many opportunities to realize the extent of the law's authority over the lives of women.

In the first half of the 1800s, women—particularly those who married—had few legal rights. A woman had no right to the guardianship of her own children: A husband could apprentice their offspring without the mother's consent, and he could even appoint another guardian to raise them in the event of his death. A married woman could not own property, and her wages belonged to her husband. Though a wife had no right of inheritance, a benevolent husband might remember her in his will. Otherwise, in New York, a widow received "all spinning wheels, weaving-looms, or stoves put up for use; the family Bible, family pictures, school-books, and books not exceeding in value $50; ten sheep and their fleeces, and the yarn and cloth manufactured from the same; one cow, two swine, and the pork of such swine; all necessary wearing apparel, beds, bedstands, and bedding; the clothing of the widow and her ornaments proper to her station; one table, six chairs, six knives and forks, six tea-cups and saucers, one sugar-dish, one milk-pot, one tea-pot, and six spoons." Since it was customary for sons to inherit their father's estate (with the request that they offer their mother a place in her former home), many women came weeping to Judge Cady.

Though the judge frequently gave them a few dollars from his own pocket, he couldn't change their situation. Elizabeth demanded an explanation. Judge Cady opened his statute books and showed her the laws. There was nothing he could do, he said.

Elizabeth grieved while the law students laughed, thinking it fun to see the judge's pretty daughter so upset. They searched through the statute books with unusual energy. When Elizabeth received new bracelets and a necklace that Christmas, Henry Bayard was prepared.

"Now," he said, "if in due time you should be my wife, those ornaments would be mine; I could take them and lock them up, and you could never wear them except with my permission. I could even exchange them for a box of cigars, and you could watch them evaporate in smoke."

Months went by and the teasing continued. Indeed, "a succession," of law students "was always coming fresh from college and full of conceit." They all enjoyed baiting Elizabeth. She marked the laws that the students teased her about in pencil, and this gave her quite an education. In time she knew by heart the numbers of the pages where these obnoxious provisions were written down. Sometimes she laughed at them, for they seemed to her too ridiculous to be taken seriously; but more often she cried.

Finally one day, Flora Campbell, a woman Elizabeth knew well, was the woman weeping in Judge Cady's office. The lament was familiar. Flora Campbell's son had inherited the family farm and had immediately begun mistreating his mother. Once again, Elizabeth heard her father say he could do nothing.

Elizabeth wanted never to hear this again. She decided to get scissors and cut the offending laws from the books. Then, she reasoned, there'd be an end to Flora Campbell's troubles.

When her father realized her intent, he called her back into the office and closed the door. Judge Cady explained to her, step by step, how the laws were proposed and passed. He told her, too, that there were many law libraries in New York. She could not destroy them all; and, even if she could, it would do no good, for the laws would not change.

"When you are grown up, and able to prepare a speech," Judge Cady continued, "you must go down to Albany and talk to the legislators; tell them all you have seen in this office . . . and if you can persuade them to pass new laws, the old ones will be a dead letter."

Elizabeth put away her scissors and left her father's library intact.

As bright and feisty as his daughter was, Daniel Cady soon lost interest in her. Eleazar, the judge's beloved, last-surviving son, died in an accident right after his graduation from Union College. Eleazar was the child upon whom Judge Cady's hopes had rested—the one who was to become a lawyer, the one who was to inherit the troublesome but treasured law library. Now he was dead, and his father thought of nothing and no one but his own grief and his lost boy.

Eleazer's wake, the time his bereaved family and other mourners kept vigil over his body, was like most 19th-century wakes. It was held at home, in the parlor. The drapes were drawn and the lights extinguished; mirrors and pictures were covered with pale cloth, eerily ghostlike in the darkened room. Elizabeth was then only 11 years old. When she entered the room, she found her father in a chair beside Eleazer's coffin. Daniel Cady neither looked up nor spoke to her. He remained absolutely still in the silence. He seemed as pale as his dead son. Finally, tentatively, Elizabeth sat on his lap and lay her head upon his shoulder. When he closed his arm around her, she was relieved. She thought her presence had comforted him.

"Oh, my daughter," he said, still looking at the casket, "I wish you were a boy!"

The young girl hugged him hard. "I will try to be all my brother was!" she tearfully promised.

How could she fill the place of a well-educated son? She was merely a daughter and had received only a dame school education. The next day she called upon the family minister, the Reverend Simon Hosack. She found him working in the garden. Reverend Hosack had always been kind to her and he was, as she knew, a well-educated man. She asked him for his help.

"My father prefers boys," she told him. "He wishes I was one, and I intend to be as near like one as possible. I am going to ride on horseback and study Greek. Will you give me a Greek lesson now? I want to begin without delay."

"Yes, child," Reverend Hosack answered, "come into my library and we will begin without delay."

Elizabeth learned Greek; she advanced in mathematics; she soared on horseback over tall fences and deep ditches. But her father was not consoled. He failed to notice his daughter's efforts. In fact, he failed to notice her company. For several months after Eleazar's burial—until winter finally froze the ground—Daniel Cady went every day to the grave. Elizabeth went with him. There, she waited between two poplar trees while her father mourned. Forgetting her, Daniel Cady would fling himself across his son's grave and sob until dark.

Elizabeth continued to do well despite her father's inattention. She entered the Johnstown Academy with the neighborhood boys and studied Latin, Greek, and mathematics. She worked hard, eager to win prizes for her father's sake. Surely, she thought, he'd notice a prize. But becoming first in her class was difficult. Many of the boys were older than her, and all wanted the prizes for themselves. When Elizabeth finally won her prize for Greek, she ran all the way to her father's office.

"There, I got it!" she shouted.

Daniel Cady (Courtesy of Rhoda Barney Jenkins)

Judge Cady was interested and, Elizabeth thought, pleased. Until, that is, he sighed a familiar sigh and told her once again, "Ah, you should have been a boy!" Writing later of Eleazar, "a young man of great talent and promise," Elizabeth could not help being bitter. She and her sisters had "early felt that this son filled a larger place in our father's affections and future plans than the five daughters together." After his death, Elizabeth, at least, was sure of it.

In the end, Reverend Hosack was more impressed than Elizabeth's father with her efforts. Left without a son, Judge Cady decided to promise his library to whatever future grandson might first become a lawyer. The reverend cared for his books, too, and, like Judge Cady, had definite thoughts about whom else might benefit from them. And so, years later, when his former friend and pupil received the sad news of his death, she also received one last gift. "My Greek lexicon, Testament, and grammar, and four volumes of Scott's Commentaries," Reverend Hosack had directed, "I will to Elizabeth Cady."

Elizabeth was not alone in trying to console Judge Cady. Margaret Cady also tried to fill Eleazar's place. At 42 years of age, she gave birth to her 11th child—a son, named Eleazar after his brother. But it was a futile effort. When the infant died before his first birthday, his mother was bereft and truly broken. She withdrew from the family to her bedroom and left the care of her four youngest daughters to her eldest, Tryphena.

Fortunately for the Cady girls, Tryphena soon married. Her husband, Edward Bayard (brother of the teasing Henry), was a handsome, fun-loving attorney of 21. He was well known to the girls, since he'd been both Eleazar's classmate and a student in their father's office. Together, he and Tryphena tried to restore a sense of joy to the household.

They largely succeeded. Edward praised Elizabeth's advances in her studies and her exploits on horseback. He (and his brother, who remained a student in Judge Cady's office) encouraged play as well as work. Childhood changed drastically for the girls. In the hands of newlyweds, this time became "an era of picnics, birthday parties, books, musical instruments, and ponies." It became, too, a time of travel.

Shortly after Eleazar's death and their own marriage, Tryphena and Edward proposed a visit to Margaret Cady's mother, Elizabeth Simpson Livingston. Livingston lived in Caanan,

New York, which was 20 miles southeast of Albany and a little over 60 miles from their own home in Johnstown. They traveled there in two horse-drawn carriages, through the beautiful Mohawk Valley and on to Caanan. For girls who'd never left Fulton County, this was a journey indeed! They marveled and cried out at the first bridges and ferry boats passed in the valley and were awed by their first sight of a city. Entering Schenectady, and then the Given's Hotel for lunch, they lost all composure, running around to look at everything.

Their mother was not amused. Fortunately, Edward Bayard was, and he gave the girls a tour around the hotel's dining room. But by the time the family reached Albany, a decision had been reached: Elizabeth, Little Madge, and Kate would eat in their rooms.

Still the children's enthusiasm could not be curtailed. Every street corner in Albany had crowds larger than those that appeared in Johnstown on Training Day. Elizabeth and her sisters leaned out the windows and stared. Between meals, they visited a museum for the first time and strolled through their state's capital city. They were still "in a whirlpool of excitement" when they finally reached Grandmother Livingston's farm.

After a wonderful week spent among aunts, uncles, cousins, and their dear grandmother, the family rearranged itself in the two carriages and retraced the path home. "When we . . . told our village companions what we had seen in our extensive travels (only seventy miles from home)," Elizabeth later wrote, "they were filled with wonder, and we became heroines in their estimation."

Elizabeth was faring well in her own estimation, too, as she passed her 14th birthday and approached her graduation from Johnstown Academy. She had not been able to console her father, but after all her hard work, she was going to graduate at the top of her class. After that, Elizabeth Cady planned to go to college.

3

EDUCATIONS: 1830–39

Elizabeth graduated from Johnstown Academy in 1830. To her astonishment, no college in America admitted female students. "Those with whom I had studied and contended for prizes for five years came to bid me good-bye," she later wrote sadly, "and I learned of the barrier that prevented me from following in their footsteps—'no girls admitted here.'" Her parents were astonished too—but only that she had any interest whatsoever in going. Surely Elizabeth understood what was required of a wealthy teenage girl in the first half of the 19th century?

It was surprisingly little: well-groomed attendance at a series of "balls and dinners," and then marriage to one of one's former dance partners. If Elizabeth wanted more, Judge Cady said, exasperated, let her learn to "make pudding and pies." Elizabeth did not agree, and she did not understand. "My vexation and mortification knew no bounds," she declared. She wanted more than pies.

The judge made a concession. He suggested that she do clerical work in his office and then accompany him on the court circuit. But Elizabeth knew she hadn't completed her education. She enlisted her brother-in-law, Edward Bayard, to argue on her side, and she continued pleading her own case. Finally, it was agreed that she would attend Emma Willard's female seminary.

Emma Hart (later, Emma Willard) had long been determined to provide higher education to women. This was especially difficult since she herself had been barred from receiving the education she wished to pass on. Her own father had recognized her intelligence; he had willingly provided her with what education he could. But soon she, like young Elizabeth Cady, reached the arbitrary barrier. She then became a teacher and, at the age of 20, took charge of the Female Academy at Middlebury, Vermont in 1807. Such female academies were the only institutions open to girls in their later teens. Actually finishing schools, they offered a curriculum of ornamental activities: embroidery, conversational French, and the polite rendering of landscapes on canvas.

When Emma Hart married, she did what was expected and left her position. She did not retreat entirely into domesticity, though. Her husband, John Willard, was a physician and a director of the Vermont State Bank. He was pleased rather than alarmed when Emma began to read his medical books, and he encouraged her when she began an independent study of geometry and natural philosophy. Then John experienced a financial reversal, and Emma quickly offered him her help.

She proposed turning some of the rooms of their large brick house into a boarding school for young women. This would both alleviate the couple's financial difficulties and give Emma the freedom to design an entirely new type of school for girls. Reluctantly, John Willard agreed.

Emma Willard's new academy had a wonderful teacher in its proprietor, but few tools. In order to teach geometry, for example, Willard had to cut fruits and vegetables into cones, spheres, pyramids, and cylinders. She continued to study on her own and began hurriedly teaching whatever she learned to students she hoped would become teachers. "I spent ten to twelve hours a day in teaching and, on extraordinary occasions such as preparing [students] for examination, fifteen," she later recalled, "besides having always under investigation some one new subject which, as I studied, I simultaneously taught a class of my ablest pupils."

The students learned and thrived. Satisfied with the results of her experiment, Emma Willard invited the professors of nearby Middlebury College to audit her students' examinations. As Ezra Brainerd, president of that college in 1893, admitted, his predecessors found "proof that 'the female mind' could apprehend the solid studies of the college course." This proof could not eliminate prejudice in 1815, however. As President Brainerd told an audience much later, Emma Willard asked, "in turn, to attend the examinations of the young men . . . It is humiliating to think that this privilege was

Emma Willard (Courtesy of Emma Willard School)

refused, President Davis considering that it would not be a safe precedent, and that it would be unbecoming for her to attend."

John Willard was more helpful. A wealthy and influential man at the time of their marriage, he'd introduced his wife to other prominent men. Some of these became benefactors of Emma Willard's school. One, General Van Schoonhoven, was a resident of New York state, which had used public monies for education since 1795. The general suggested that the Willards relocate to his hometown of Waterford, New York, and petition the state legislature for funds to help in establishing another women's school. Soon after her rebuff by President Davis of Middlebury College, Emma Willard asked for and received her husband's support of such a venture. The couple moved to Waterford, and Emma Willard began to write her proposal.

One of the hardest decisions was just what to call this new type of school. Explaining both the difficulty and the solution, she wrote that she finally heard "someone pray for 'our seminary of learning' . . . that word, while it is high as the highest, is also low as the lowest, and will not create a jealousy that we mean to intrude upon the province of men." In 1819, she completed a far-reaching proposal for a drastic change in women's education. It contained a description of what would become known, not as a female academy or college, but as a "female seminary."

"An Address to the Public; Particularly to the Members of the Legislature of New York, Proposing a Plan for Improving Female Education" was presented to Governor DeWitt Clinton and the legislature in Albany, New York. Although Emma Willard couldn't address the legislature herself (American women were not permitted to speak in public in 1819), she appealed to legislators one at a time. Her proposal passed, and she was granted a charter, that is, a legal document authorizing her to set up a women's school. When neither the state legislature nor the town of Waterford appropriated funds, the citizens of Troy, New York, offered to raise the necessary money. Soon Emma Willard wrote, "that city has raised $4,000 by tax and another fund has been raised by subscription. They are now erecting a brick building 60' x 40', three stories from the basement; and the basement, raised 5' above the ground, contains a dining room as well as a kitchen and a laundry."

The Troy Female Seminary had been open just 10 years when Elizabeth Cady entered its doors in 1831. She was about to receive the very best education available to a young woman, and she knew it. She was disappointed anyway. "I had fixed my mind on Union College," she explained. She knew there would be a great difference between a young men's college and even the most advanced female seminary.

There had been a lot of resistance to the idea of increased education of any sort for women. In order to overcome it, Emma Willard had claimed that education would help women to be better wives and mothers. Among other things, she said, education would enable mothers to prepare sons for voting citizenship. This argument finally allayed the fear that educated women might abandon traditional responsibilities. But it also left those traditional expectations unchallenged and—worse, in Elizabeth's eyes—in evidence all through the curriculum at Troy. Domestic arts were taught along with science, mathematics, logic, and literature. And these last college courses were taught with a limiting deference to ladylike modesty.

In the early 1830s, for example, no lady would publicly mention the body she possessed. Prudery was so extreme that young women were encouraged to change their underclothes while still wearing their nightgowns, thus protecting themselves from the "shocking" sight of their own bodies. It was in this climate that Emma Willard tried to teach physiology. But, as one of her biographers describes, "[m]others visiting a class at the Seminary . . . were so shocked at the sight of a pupil drawing heart, arteries and veins on a blackboard to explain the circulation of the blood, that they left the room in shame and dismay." The human body was subsequently covered over with cardboard in all of the Seminary's textbooks.

Other subjects were taught more successfully. As in her Vermont school, Willard herself created some of the necessary tools. These now included textbooks. In 1822, the year after her school opened, she wrote *A System of Universal Geography on the Principles of Comparison and Classification* with William Channing Woodbridge. Unlike other geographies then in use, hers did not treat London as the world's center. It was considered groundbreaking. In 1828, she completed the first of her history texts, *Republic of America*. Her account of the American Revolution was applauded by no less an authority than Lafayette, and it was the history text Daniel Webster, famous New England lawyer and senator, relied on: "I keep it near me as a book of reference, accurate in facts and dates," he said.

Elizabeth admired her teacher, "a splendid-looking woman," as she described her, "then in her prime." In Willard's school she studied Greek, French, logic, algebra and geometry, and modern history. Fifty years later, as one of the editors of the *History of Woman Suffrage*, she would place Emma Willard in the first chapter, at the very beginning of woman's struggle for equality: as a force in the destiny not only of Elizabeth Cady Stanton but of all American women.

Elizabeth graduated from the Troy Female Seminary in 1833. Proud to call herself an alumna, she returned to her parents' home. She was 17 years old. It was time for her to be married. But to whom?

Girls from less prosperous families might have worked while they wondered. Their choice of occupation would have been one of these: teaching, factory work, domestic service, or sewing. But for a young woman of Elizabeth's background, the time between schooling and marriage was spent dancing. Elizabeth was no exception.

Her hair was still curly and her skin still pink and fair. Quick to laugh and light on her feet, Elizabeth loved this time, as she put it, "of irrepressible joy and freedom." She danced; she went on sleigh rides; she rode on horseback through many a Mohawk Valley sunrise. But she did not marry; at least, not right away. Instead, Elizabeth found a way to extend her education further. She did her dancing in Peterboro, New York, at the home of her cousin, Gerrit Smith.

Gerrit Smith was the son of Margaret Cady's sister Elizabeth, and her husband, Peter Smith. Like his cousin, he was related through his mother to the Livingston family, part of New York's old aristocracy. From his father, he received one of New York state's largest personal fortunes. Peter Smith had been partners with John Jacob Astor. Astor, a poor, 21-year-old immigrant in 1784, became, by the end of his life, the richest man in America. Astor and Smith made their fortunes in the fur trade—at the time, a beaver skin purchased for $1.00 from a New York Native American could be resold for $6.25 in London—and from land speculation. Their first purchase was 37,200 acres in the Mohawk Valley; at one point, Peter Smith alone owned more than 60,000 acres in central New York State. When Gerrit was nine years old, his father moved the family from Utica to a new home on these lands in Madison County. He founded a town there and named it Smithfield; then he founded a village nearby and named it Peterboro; and then he built his house.

The son who inherited this tremendous fortune was an abolitionist, committed not to respect and obey the laws upholding slavery but to abolish them. Both Gerrit Smith and his wife, Ann Fitzhugh Smith, felt this way. They turned their Peterboro mansion into a gathering place for abolitionist activities. Elizabeth was a good friend of the Smiths' daughter, Elizabeth (known as "Libby"), and frequently traveled through the Mohawk Valley to visit her in Peterboro. There, at the western extremity of the Adirondack Mountains, Elizabeth Cady found her world expanded. "Every member of their household is a abolitionist, even to the coachman," she soon realized. Moreover, every member of the household, along with every guest, was involved in a loud and ongoing discussion of the day's reform movements. "The youngest of us," Elizabeth eventually wrote both of herself and others, "felt that the conclusions reached in this school of philosophy were not to be questioned."

This was not the first time Elizabeth had thought about slavery or even the injustices faced by free African-Americans in her own home. One of the Cady family's black servants, Peter Teabout, had been especially kind to the Cady children. He was the only black member of the local Episcopal church, which nonetheless had an entire pew set aside for blacks. The Cady children, when young, attended church with Peter. Whenever the sexton tried to seat them in a "white pew," they refused. They always sat in the "Negro pew" with Peter, instead. Even so, he still had to wait for all the white Christians to receive communion (a sacramental taking of bread and wine) and then go himself, alone and last. But one Christmas morning, Elizabeth watched her youngest sister with pride. Little Kate, as she was known by then, saw her friend Peter alone at the altar once more. She left her seat, walked calmly to his side, and took his hand. "What a lesson," Elizabeth wrote, "to that prejudiced congregation!"

At Peterboro, though, Elizabeth would receive lessons in the meaning of racial injustice far in advance of any lessons she had learned as a child. One day, Elizabeth and others of the Smiths' young cousins were talking easily among themselves in the parlor. Gerrit walked quietly into the room and gave instructions that Elizabeth Cady Stanton later recounted in her autobiography.

"I have a most important secret to tell you, which you must keep to yourselves religiously for twenty-four hours," he said.

They promised, one at a time. Finally, their cousin Gerrit was satisfied that they were bound.

"Now," he continued, "follow me to the third story."

They did, quickly and quietly. When their cousin opened the door to a large room, they saw inside a "beautiful quadroon girl," a teenager like themselves.

"Harriet," Gerrit Smith addressed her, "I have brought all my young cousins to see you. I want you to make good abolitionists of them by telling them the history of your life—what you have seen and suffered in slavery."

He then told his cousins: "Harriet has just escaped from her master, who is visiting in Syracuse, and is on her way to Canada. She will start this evening and you may never have another opportunity of seeing a slave girl face to face, so ask her all you care to know of the system of slavery."

Harriet spoke to them candidly. A "quadroon" slave, she was but one-quarter black. This meant that her mother and her grandmother before her were each impregnated by white men. Though Harriet didn't say, such men were usually the owners of the childbearing women, or male members of the owner's family. And, though no court would recognize it as a crime at the time, it was usually rape that resulted in these pregnancies.

Harriet herself was "sold for her beauty in a New Orleans market when but fourteen years of age"—quite possibly by her own father. Whatever she told Elizabeth Cady and her cousins about her life after 14 was horrible. It made them weep. Even 60 years later, when she wrote her autobiography, Elizabeth chose not to enumerate the details. "The fate of such girls is too well known," she commented bitterly, "to need rehearsal." The knowledge of such a fate was new to her that day, however; she listened and spoke to Harriet for two hours.

From that time on, Elizabeth called herself an "earnest abolitionist." She watched with a full heart as Harriet left the house. It was now dusk, and the young girl was dressed in the simple gray and white clothing worn by Quaker women. With one of the abolitionist coachmen, Harriet left by carriage for Oswego. If she arrived there safely, she'd be hidden again and then ferried across the lake to the Canadian shore. She'd be on her own, then—but free.

The Smiths and their guests remained at home and continued chatting and dining in their usual way. They knew that Harriet's master would be following her with federal marshals, and that they might well trace her to Peterboro. If they did, it was important that everything seem ordinary.

When they arrived the next day, Gerrit Smith asked them in. To Elizabeth's further surprise, he then invited them to search the house and join the family for dinner!

Harriet's master and the federal marshals, satisfied that she was not there, joined the Smiths at their table. Elizabeth was impressed by her cousin's willingness to explain his views even to those least likely to understand or agree. She was not alone. The unexpected dinner guests were "surprised to find an abolitionist so courteous and affable." All through dinner, while the debate continued, Harriet's carriage traveled further from Peterboro. She was more than 20 hours ahead of the marshals when the chase resumed.

When the coachman returned, saying Harriet was safely in Canada, there was a celebration in Peterboro. Gerrit Smith decided to make it a public one. He published an open letter in the *New York Tribune*, addressed to Harriet's former master. He told his one-time dinner guest "that he would no doubt rejoice to know that his slave Harriet, in whose fate he felt so deep an interest, was now a free woman, safe under the shadow of the British throne. I had the honor of entertaining her under my roof, sending her in my carriage to Lake Ontario, just eighteen hours before your arrival; hence my willingness to have you search my premises."

The search party had, at least, found high spirits in Peterboro. These were not feigned. More than any other environment of her younger years, Elizabeth appreciated this one. "There never was such an atmosphere of love and peace, of freedom and good cheer, in any other home I visited," she later wrote. In that easy, happy place, she found "a new inspiration in life and . . . new ideas of individual rights."

She'd also begun to find a way to live. In Peterboro, Elizabeth was in constant contact with reformers of every persuasion: abolitionists, temperance workers, philanthropists, and religious reformers. All seemed happier in their commitment than others had ever seemed in their leisure. "Peterboro made social life seem tame and profitless elsewhere," Elizabeth realized. She felt drawn to the idea of an active life: to a life that somehow mattered.

Elizabeth Cady Stanton at age 20 (Courtesy of Brigham Young University Photoarchives)

She soon found herself drawn, as well, to another of Gerrit Smith's guests. His name was Henry B. Stanton. He was 10 years her senior and an abolitionist hero, "the most eloquent and impassioned orator on the anti-slavery platform." Though Henry Stanton's speeches drew rioters as well as admirers, he always said what he'd come to say. When Elizabeth heard him speak at an antislavery convention in Madison County, she saw him bring his audience to tears; when she met him at her cousin's home, she found him "remarkable."

He was tall, handsome and, Elizabeth believed, engaged to marry. Since she thought he was quite removed from any possibility of romance, her behavior with him was "free and easy." Henry Stanton joined Elizabeth, Libby, and others at antislavery conventions in Madison County and back at the fireside in Peterboro for long, unguarded conversation. "It seemed to me," Elizabeth remembered later, "that I never had so much happiness crowded into one short month." She was in love. She was also mistaken about Henry Stanton's engagement.

He approached her alone one morning and asked her to go for a horseback ride. They rode for a long distance, pausing here and there to admire the landscape and, Elizabeth wrote, "perchance, each other." When Henry B. Stanton proposed marriage to Elizabeth Cady, she accepted—"with mingled emotions of pleasure and astonishment."

Elizabeth was now 24 and had been urged for many years to marry. But Henry Stanton was not the suitor her parents had had in mind. Their nephew, Gerrit Smith, realized this as soon as the young couple announced their news. Eager to discuss abolitionism with federal marshals and pursuing masters, Gerrit Smith was dismayed by the thought of discussing Elizabeth's courtship and engagement with his conservative uncle. He called his cousin into the library.

Elizabeth found the ensuing discussion to be one of her life's most confusing. Though her cousin Gerrit admired Henry Stanton, he thought Elizabeth should consider breaking her engagement. First he said that Judge Cady would never allow his daughter to marry Henry Stanton. Then he outlined the difficulties with marriage in general: the legal disabilities it imposed upon women and, if one chose in haste, the possibility for deeply felt sorrow. Elizabeth had been courted and became engaged while a guest in his home, Gerrit Smith acknowledged. But he would accept no responsibility for her actions if she refused to follow his advice.

Elizabeth did not follow her cousin's advice, and he did not send her home. Instead, he allowed her to remain in Peterboro while she informed her family by letter of her engagement. Judge Cady was "even more indignant at my cousin than at me," Elizabeth decided. Thinking her family had accommodated itself to her plans, she returned home.

There was no accommodation. Those who had always described marriage "in dazzling colors" were furious over her engagement. Everything she'd ever learned as a young girl in her father's office, she learned again. Marriage was described as a state "beset with dangers and disappointments." And men, she was assured, were "depraved and unreliable." Miserable, she broke her engagement.

Henry Stanton accepted that there were now no formal plans to wed. But he did not accept an end to the courtship. "A happy new year to thee, my own beloved Elizabeth!" he'd written on the first day of 1840. "I hope this bright but cold morning finds thee cheerful and brilliant as usual, and encircled with the affectionate admiration of many warm friends. But, among them all thou shalt not find one who loves thee more devotedly, or would do more to render this and all thy future years happy

Henry B. Stanton (Courtesy New-York Historical Society, N.Y., and Rhoda Barney Jenkins)

than him whose hand traces these lines." He continued to write in this loving manner even after the engagement ended.

Though she was forbidden, Elizabeth answered Henry Stanton's letters. Some, he may have intended for Elizabeth's parents' eyes as well as her own. "I have never received a dollar's gratuitous aid from anyone," wrote Judge Cady's would-be son-in-law, "though it has been frequently pressed upon me. I always declined it . . . because I was aware that if I would be a man, I must build my own foundation with my own hands."

Even without such a letter, Elizabeth was sure Henry Stanton wasn't a fortune hunter. Nor did she believe him to be depraved and unreliable.

And the state of matrimony described in the law was, perhaps, not fixed. Emma Willard had not been the only woman crusading for change during Elizabeth's teens and early twenties. In 1836, the New York state legislature had been petitioned (though unsuccessfully) to create the Married Women's Property Act and expand women's rights. By the later 1830s abolitionist women were also attracting notice. Newspapers and ministers condemned them, but these women now spoke about their beliefs in public.

Elizabeth also knew that some of these ideas were finding their way into at least some marriages. Just the year before, Henry Stanton had attended the wedding of his abolitionist colleagues Angelina Grimké and Theodore Weld; it was this couple who'd first omitted the bride's customary pledge "to obey."

In any event, Elizabeth hoped that the marriage she contemplated might be even more than a love match. Henry hoped so, too. Judge Cady had by now threatened to disinherit his daughter if she continued to encourage her abolitionist suitor. Elizabeth accepted that, but she would disavow neither Henry nor the abolitionist cause. The couple fully expected that such reform would be part and parcel of their marriage, of their attempt to build a meaningful life together. As Henry wrote to a friend, his beloved had "wedded her soul to the cause of duty"—to a cause as well as to a husband.

So she had. At the end of April 1840, Henry Stanton prepared to sail for London as a delegate to the World Anti-Slavery Convention. And the girl who'd marveled at a trip to Canaan packed her bags to cross an ocean.

4

CROSSING MORE THAN AN OCEAN: 1840–48

On Christmas Eve, 1840, Elizabeth Cady Stanton and Henry B. Stanton returned from their activist honeymoon. Elizabeth, disembarking in New York City, was thrilled to be in America again. "It seemed to me," she wrote, "that the sky was clearer, the air more refreshing, and the sunlight more brilliant than in any other land!" It was a country whose opinion of women she'd vowed to change. "A convention," she and Lucretia Mott had promised each other, "as soon as we return home." But as it turned out, Elizabeth Cady Stanton was to do, and learn, a few other things first.

Her immediate desire was to be reunited with her family. There was no lingering disagreement between Elizabeth and her sister Harriet Eaton—they'd been smiling when they said good-bye on the day of Elizabeth and Henry's departure for London. Now, the returning newlyweds joined Harriet's family in celebrating Christmas and New Year's Day. It was a wonderful, week-long visit. But Elizabeth knew her parents, and any hope of reconciliation, waited in Johnstown. Right after the holidays, she and Henry left the Eatons' Manhattan home.

It was the very beginning of 1841, and snowy. Horse-drawn sleighs carried them over the first and last parts of the journey; the middle stretch, between Albany and Schenectady, they covered by rail. Although Elizabeth was still in holiday spirits, she must have wondered what kind of reception she and her husband would receive. While on her honeymoon, she'd written to her parents many times. She loved Henry Stanton and them as well; could they, after all, understand and accept her marriage?

To her relief, they could. Daniel and Margaret Cady welcomed their daughter and son-in-law with enthusiasm and warmth and then gave more than simple good wishes. Judge Cady offered Henry a place in his office and the opportunity to study law. And Margaret Cady, much recovered from her depression of a decade prior, joined her husband in another generous offer: Elizabeth and Henry might live with them until Henry passed the bar.

Two very happy years followed. Elizabeth was pleased to see a mutual respect begin to grow between her father and her husband. Soon, she was able to confide to her cousin Libby Smith that "Papa seems quite contented with [Henry]." Her own feeling for Stanton she described simply, but emphatically, as her "great love for Henry."

Moreover, Henry and Elizabeth were accepted into the Cady household on their own terms. Henry studied, but he also continued his political activities. He made about 16 speeches a month during his first summer in the judge's office and, before long, was made a member of the Liberty party's central committee in New York state. For Elizabeth, too, these were "profitable years," spent "reading law, history, and political economy, with occasional interruptions to take part in some temperance or anti-slavery excitement."

She also instructed black children in the local Sunday school. Another Johnstown woman, Eliza Murray, did the same. Elizabeth had wished, upon her return from the reform circles of London, to find evidence of "social upheavals" in her birthplace. But during the planning of a church festival she realized that, at least in one regard, Johnstown had not changed.

Elizabeth's Sunday school students were tremendously excited about the festival. They were told to expect speeches in their church, all kinds of entertainment afterward, and—best of all—a starring part in the processional. Children and teachers alike prepared eagerly for the event. But when the morning finally arrived, Cady Stanton and Murray were approached by the festival's planners. These "narrow-minded bigots," as Elizabeth described them, "all church members in good standing," said that no black children were welcome in the procession or in any part of the celebration.

Cady Stanton and Murray immediately fought back, refusing, as Cady Stanton later put it, to "cater to any of these contemptible prejudices against color." The two women gathered the students to their side and would not be parted from them. Finally, they accepted a compromise. Like Peter years before, these children might walk down the church aisle, so long as their group walked last and alone.

The African-American students, unaware of the whispered argument, lined up behind the white students and marched proudly toward the church door. Then, as the last white child disappeared into the church, the doors were slammed and locked.

Outside, the black children cried and asked for an explanation. Cady Stanton and Murray told them the truth, feeling as ashamed as if they themselves had slammed the door. Though they took the children to Judge Cady's house to play, they knew they could not undo the injury. Nor could Elizabeth continue to believe that Sunday school was of real benefit to these children. Immediately after this episode, she resigned her position as their teacher.

Other events during this newlywed period were of a familial nature. On March 2, 1842, the first of Henry Stanton and Elizabeth Cady Stanton's children was born. A son, he was named Daniel Cady Stanton, in honor of Elizabeth's father.

Elizabeth was well aware of the high infant mortality rate and knew from her mother's experiences how devastating such losses were. "Having gone through the ordeal of bearing a child," she recalled, "I was determined, if possible, to keep him." Within the first two weeks of Daniel's life, his young mother read all the available child-rearing literature. Unfortunately, few of the recommended practices made sense to her. The advice of only one physician, Andrew Combe, seemed promising; Elizabeth thought he "could tell, at least, as much of babies as naturalists could of beetles and bees." She decided to adopt some of his recommendations.

Nurses in those years usually bound babies so tightly in swaddling clothes that it seemed they had been bandaged instead of dressed. The nurse hired by the Cadys for their grandson was no exception. Elizabeth thought Daniel would be more comfortable in a pillowcase, and she asked the nurse to "dress" the baby in one. The nurse refused.

After a long discussion, a compromise of sorts was reached: The nurse continued to bandage Daniel each day, and Elizabeth just as promptly freed him.

Concerned as she was that her baby not die, she was nonetheless a happy and remarkably self-confident mother. She breast-fed her baby every two hours and banned the usual herbal mixtures in between. She had the baby's mouth washed with clear water twice daily to prevent infection, and threw open wide the windows of the nursery. "I had been thinking, reading, observing," she said, "and had as little faith in the popular theories in regard to babies as on any other subject." There seemed little reason to have faith in them; Daniel's experienced nurse had lost five of her own 10 children in infancy.

Regrettably, Daniel's physicians were the Drs. Childs and Clark, and not the Dr. Combe Elizabeth so admired. Four days after Daniel's birth, it became apparent that the infant's collarbone was badly positioned. Both doctors bandaged his shoulder, but Elizabeth was pleased with neither attempt; one had turned the baby's hand blue, while the second squeezed his fingers until they were purple. She decided to care for the infant on her own. As she wrote to Henry " . . . with my usual conceit, I removed both [bandages] successfully and turned surgeon myself. I first rubbed the arm and shoulder well with arnica [a liniment made of the herb and some alcohol], then put a wet compress on the collarbone, some cotton batting rolled in linen under the arm, and over the shoulder two bands of linen, like suspenders, pinned to the belly band. This we removed night and morning, washed the shoulder with cold water and arnica and wet the compress anew. The surgeons pronounced my work all very good, and this morning the child is dressed for the first time in ten days. I did not write to you about the bandaging until I felt sure I had done well. You know it is a great thing to impress husbands . . . with the belief that their wives are indeed wonderful women!"

The doctors might have pronounced her work all very good. But they were also patronizing toward her, and jested that it was a "mother's instinct" that sometimes surpassed "a man's reason."

Elizabeth was offended: "Thank you gentlemen, there was no instinct about it," she told the doctors. "I did some hard thinking before I saw how I could get a pressure on the shoulder without impeding the circulation, as you did."

She soon had many other opportunities to set her own standards. In 1842, Henry completed his studies and decided to practice law in Boston. The family moved, and Elizabeth set up housekeeping on her own for the very first time. She gloried in it. "It is a proud moment in a woman's life to reign supreme within four walls," she recalled. And reign supreme she did. Right after their arrival in Boston, Henry told her that she'd have to oversee the domestic side of their life alone, while he built his practice. In the beginning, she viewed this more as an adventure than a burden. "Even washing day—the day so many people dread—had its charms for me," she wrote. Though two servants worked in her home, Elizabeth turned her attention to every detail. She finally learned to "make pudding and pies" and even to pickle; she attended to the flatware, china, and table linens, and made sure that even the firewood outside the door was neatly piled. "I put my soul into everything," she remembered, "and hence enjoyed it."

By the end of 1845, she and Henry had three boys, all healthy and strong. Elizabeth enjoyed motherhood and continued to bring her own ideas to it. Her children received loose clothing, regular naps, fresh air, and more than the usual amount of exercise. On laundry day, their dinner was a simple picnic out of doors. And, running or crawling about, they were called by casual nicknames: Daniel became "Niel"; Henry B. Stanton, Jr., "Kit"; and Gerrit Smith Stanton, "Gat."

But even as she supervised her children, Cady Stanton continued to read. And, at night, when the boys were safely sleeping, she and Henry entertained guests. Their circle of friends included the poet John Greenleaf Whittier; writers Lydia Maria Child and Ralph Waldo Emerson; abolitionists Abbey Kelley and Stephen Foster (who were later married); and Cady Stanton's still-radical cousin, Gerrit Smith. They also entertained William Lloyd Garrison—a hero to Cady Stanton ever since he joined the ousted women behind the curtain in London—and Frederick Douglass, whose name she had invoked while trapped behind that curtain herself. The conversations Elizabeth had with these people—"many of the noble men and women among reformers," as she described them— were inspiring, and not just to the young woman.

Frederick Douglass had been born a slave in Maryland in February 1818. The exact date of his birth and even the identity of his father was unknown to Douglass, but he always remembered the cruelty he'd witnessed as a child. Once, for example, he saw the overseer William Sevier "whip a woman, causing the blood to run half an hour at a time; and this, too, in the midst of her crying children, pleading for their mother's release." In the autumn of 1838, Douglass escaped to freedom in the North. There, he quickly became one of the abolitionist movement's most powerful orators, giving firsthand accounts of slavery that moved people as no imagined account could. He and Elizabeth Cady Stanton first met at a dinner party in Boston. He found her, he wrote later, "at pains of setting before me in a very strong light the wrong and injustice" of women's exclusion from public life. "I could not meet her arguments except with the shallow plea of 'custom,' 'natural division of duties,' 'indelicacy of woman's taking part in politics,' the common talk of 'woman's sphere,' and the like, all of which that able woman brushed away . . ." As Douglass wrote to her many years later, from the time of "that conversation with you I have been convinced of the wisdom of woman suffrage . . ."

Certainly, Elizabeth's ambitions for women, solidified at that antislavery convention in 1840, had not been forgotten. Early in her marriage, she decided she wouldn't accompany Henry to any of his antislavery meetings—not because she didn't support him or abolitionism, but because his organization had made it clear in London that women's voices would be disregarded. She remained dissatisfied with women's lives even during her own first carefree years of marriage. "The more I think on the present condition of woman," she wrote to Lucretia Mott in 1841, "the more I am oppressed with the reality of her degradation."

Her consideration of women's position was both practical and analytical. She hoped for dress reform as early as 1844 and corresponded with Lydia Maria Child about it. And, with what would become her usual precision, she carefully traced another custom to its source. One spring evening, she spoke with her friend Rebecca Eyster about married women bearing their husbands' names. Failing to convince Rebecca that this was degrading, Elizabeth continued the discussion by letter the next day.

I have very serious objections, dear Rebecca, to being called Henry. There is a great deal in a name. It often signifies much, and may involve great principle. Ask our colored brethren if there is nothing in a name. Why are the slaves nameless unless they take that of their master? Simply because they have no independent existence. They are mere chattels, with no civil or social rights. Our colored friends in this country who have education and family ties take to themselves names. Even so with women. The custom of calling women Mrs. John This and Mrs. Tom That, and colored men Sambo and Zip Coon, is founded on the principle that white men are lords of all. I cannot acknowledge this principle as just; therefore, I cannot bear the name of another.

Already, Elizabeth was beginning to see the negation of women's rights as parallel, and equal, to the negations of rights more visibly suffered by others. She acted on her convictions.

In 1836, the New York state legislature had received a petition requesting that married women be allowed to own property. Ernestine L. Rose, a Jewish woman originally from Poland, prepared the petition. By her own description, she was "a rebel at the age of five." When she was 16 and still living in Poland, her mother died. Although the estate was left to Ernestine, the girl's father promised it all to the son-in-law of his choice. Outraged, the rebel daughter sued her father. She was granted her inheritance and her freedom. She gave the money to her father after all and emigrated to America with her freedom. But once in the United States, she was disturbed by American laws concerning women. She became even more disturbed when she tried to change those laws: In 1836, she could find only five women willing to sign her petition. She added her own signature and sent it anyway.

By the time Elizabeth Cady Stanton returned to New York in 1840, Rose's petition to the state legislature had become an annual event. Cady Stanton had never forgotten Flora Campbell's sobs in Judge Cady's office and had begun to see injustice toward women in other places. She gladly circulated petitions in New York state even after her move to Boston, and lobbied in the state capital as well. So frequently was she in Albany between 1843 and 1845 that her second child, Henry, was born there. (The fact that her parents now had a town house in Albany made these trips—and childbirth away from home—easier than they might otherwise have been.) Finally, on April 6, 1848, the Married Women's Property Act was passed, and New York became the first state in which a married woman could own property.

By then, Cady Stanton's understanding of women's situation had deepened significantly. Before 1847, her examination of women's rights and wrongs had focused primarily on women's life—or lack of it—in the public realm. She knew that women suffered because colleges and professions were closed to them and because they suffered a legal death upon marriage. But she hadn't really examined women's lives within marriage; nowhere among her papers, for example, does she indicate that she ever wondered about her mother's demonstrably difficult, if upper-class, life. It wasn't until Cady Stanton was in her early thirties that consideration of this subject—a woman's daily life within the privacy of marriage—became urgent to her.

For reasons that remain unclear, Henry Stanton decided that he and Elizabeth should leave Boston. In 1847, their family resettled in the town of Seneca Falls, New York, in a house purchased for them by Judge Cady. (He placed the title in Elizabeth's name even though he knew his daughter a married woman, could not legally own it. The house became hers the following year, upon passage of the Married Women's Property Act.) Seneca Falls, called Sha-se-onse ("running or swift waters") by its original Seneca Indian residents, lies far to the west of Johnstown. It is in the beautiful Finger Lakes region of New York state, between the northern tips of the Cayuga and Seneca lakes and just south of the Erie Canal (to which it is joined by the Cayuga and Seneca canals). In the 1840s, there were about 400 homes in Seneca Falls, as well as one academy, six churches, and 20 stores. There were also two dozen small manufacturing concerns, all of which used the water power supplied by the 50 foot fall in the Seneca River. Like other villages and towns alongside the Erie Canal, Seneca Falls sent its products—lumber, plaster, leather goods, and tools—to the West. But the Erie Canal was not Seneca Falls' only link to larger cities: One could travel east to Syracuse or northwest to Rochester by rail.

Nevertheless, the move from city to country changed Elizabeth's life immediately and drastically. She wrote in her autobiography:

> In Seneca Falls my life was comparatively solitary, and the change from Boston was somewhat depressing. There [in Boston], all my immediate friends were reformers, I had near neighbors, a new home with all the modern conveniences, and well-trained servants. Here our residence was on the outskirts of town, roads very often muddy and no sidewalks most of the way, Mr. Stanton was frequently from home, I had poor servants, and an increasing number of children. To keep a house and grounds in good order, purchase every article for daily use, keep the wardrobes of half a dozen human beings in proper trim, take the children to dentists, shoemakers, and different schools, or find teachers at home, altogether made sufficient work to keep one brain busy, as well as all the hands I could impress into service.

Things that had seemed small conveniences in Boston were now seen as the great timesavers they were. In 1847, city women could buy most foods at market and have ice delivered; their country counterparts, Elizabeth Cady Stanton now among them, had to grow much of their own food and then find ways to keep it fresh without ice. These women spent many

East View of Seneca Falls Village (1841 engraving from Henry Stowell, *A History of Seneca Falls, New York, 1779–1862*)

hours in the garden, and many more hours canning, salting, and otherwise preserving food in hot kitchens without running water. Lydia Maria Child, frequent guest in Cady Stanton's Boston home, was author of many housekeeping books as well as editor of the *Anti-Slavery Standard.* A glance at Child's *The American Frugal Housewife* gives some idea of the labor involved in storing food:

> Eggs will keep almost any length of time in lime-water properly prepared. One pint of coarse salt, and one pint of unslacked lime, to a pailful of water. If there be too much lime, it will eat the shells from the eggs; and if there be a single egg cracked, it will spoil the whole. They should be covered with lime-water, and kept in a cold place. The yolk becomes slightly red; but I have seen eggs, thus kept, perfectly sweet and fresh at the end of three years . . . If you have a greater quantity of cheeses in the house than is likely to be soon used, cover them carefully with paper fastened on with flour paste, so as to exclude the air. In this way they may be kept free from insects for years . . . Cabbages put into a hole in the ground will keep well during the winter, and be hard, fresh, and sweet, in the spring. Many farmers keep potatoes in the same way . . . For curing hams . . . rub them with salt very thoroughly, and let them lay twenty-four hours. To each ham allow two ounces of salt-petre, one quart of common salt and one quart of molasses. First baste them with molasses; next rub in the salt-petre; and, last of all, the common salt. They must be carefully turned and rubbed every day for six weeks; then hang them in a chimney, or a smoke-house, for four weeks. They should be well covered up in paper bags, and put in a chest, or barrel, with layers of ashes, or charcoal, between. When you take out a ham to cut for use, be sure to put it away in a dark place, well covered up, especially in summer . . .

Elizabeth may have been unhappy with these new responsibilities, but she managed them well. At least one neighbor praised the "large garden and fruit trees" and the "constant supply of canned goods and preserves on hand" in her household.

But if the physical work was exhausting, the growing loneliness was worse. Elizabeth and Henry had been less and less often together as the years passed. Elizabeth had given birth to Henry's namesake without him, in Albany. Two years earlier, during Daniel's birth, Henry had been away on antislavery business. Soon after, he began to travel on legal as well as political business; he also pursued elective office. By the time the family moved to Seneca Falls, Henry was home for only about three months of every year.

Without question, it was extremely difficult for him to support his family and, at the same time, to continue his work as an abolitionist. When another abolitionist pointed to Judge Cady's wealth as a possible source of income, Stanton was annoyed: "True, my father-in-law is worth some property; but he does not give his sons-in-law a dollar and will not until he dies, except to keep them from starving, thinking it better . . . to aid them indirectly by throwing business their way, and thus make them climb up as he did, by their own strength." It's also clear that the marriage was important to Henry and that he regretted his frequent absence. During separations, he'd always taken more care than Elizabeth to stay in touch. "If you knew how happy it makes me feel to get a letter from you," he wrote during one of their first separations, "you would not let a fortnight pass away without writing to me. Two weeks today since I heard from you!"

His letters were the same frequent, loving letters that had advanced their furtive courtship: "Last night I dreamed of being with you. Oh how very sorry was I when I awoke and found it was but a dream! I do think of you very, very often: and I long to be with you again, to enjoy your smile and kisses . . . Write to me, dear love, every week. For I delight to hear from you. Ah, verily, Henry."

Elizabeth chose not to write every week.

She was proud of Henry's commitment to the abolitionist cause. Of all the volumes in her library, the one she most cherished was John Greenleaf Whittier's first book of poetry. She prized it not for any one poem, but for its dedication "to Henry B. Stanton, as a token of the author's personal friendship, and of his respect for the unreserved devotion of exalted talents to the cause of humanity and freedom." But she no longer felt herself included in the cause of humanity and freedom so important to her husband.

She saw the similarity between a slave's existence and her own. The abolitionist Henry Stanton did not. He traveled widely, doing his chosen work, while his wife—at home and essentially alone—did only what was necessary for the daily subsistence of others.

She would always remember this as the time when "the real struggle was upon me." And what the struggle consisted of was this: learning to understand that neither intelligence nor education, wealthy father nor reformer husband, was sufficient to protect a woman from a domestic destiny. She'd never wanted what was considered a woman's normal life and she knew she'd fought hard to avoid it. In London, in Albany, in Boston, it seemed she'd won. Now she realized that she'd made only a temporary exception of herself.

This was one of the loneliest and hardest times of her life. And yet, in her solitary plight, she began to identify even more strongly than before with other women. By the end of her first year in Seneca Falls, she knew she was willing to fight for change—not only for herself, but for all women.

> The general discontent I felt with woman's portion as wife, mother, housekeeper, physician, and spiritual guide, the chaotic conditions into which everything fell without her constant supervision, and the wearied, anxious look of the majority of women impressed me with a strong feeling that some active measures should be taken to remedy the wrongs of society in general, and of women in particular. My experience at the World's Anti-Slavery Convention, all that I had read of the legal status of women, and the oppression I saw everywhere, together swept across my soul, intensified now by many personal experiences. It seemed to me as if all the elements had conspired to impel me to some onward step.

5

KEEPING PROMISES: 1848–54

In July 1848, Lucretia and James Mott were visiting Lucretia's sister, Martha Coffin Wright, in Auburn, New York, not too far from Seneca Falls. Jane Hunt, a Quaker and friend of both sisters, invited them to tea at her home in Waterloo on Thursday, July 13; she said that Elizabeth Cady Stanton and another woman, Mary Ann M'Clintock, would also be there. The invitation was accepted, and Lucretia Mott began to look forward to seeing Elizabeth Cady Stanton once again.

The two women had not seen each other since the World Anti-Slavery Convention, and they greeted each other warmly. Over tea, Cady Stanton spoke of her married life to Mott and the other women. Cady Stanton "poured out . . . ," as she remembered later, "the torrent of my long-accumulating discontent with such vehemence and indignation that I stirred myself, as well as the rest of the party, to do and dare anything." The vow made in London had not been forgotten. Now, moved by Cady Stanton's recounting of her experiences, Martha Coffin Wright, Jane Hunt, and Mary Ann M'Clintock also wanted to act. And so, the five agreed to do the near impossible: They'd hold a women's rights convention within the week. That very afternoon, notice was delivered to the *Seneca Falls Courier* and use of the Wesleyan Chapel in Seneca Falls arranged.

On Sunday the women re-assembled, this time in M'Clintock's parlor. They had only three days left to prepare for the convention. First, they studied summaries of male temperance and antislavery organizations, hoping to find a ready model for their undertaking. They rejected them all as "too tame and pacific" for what the women hoped would be "the inauguration of a rebellion such as the world has never before seen." Then one woman began to read a document that perfectly stated

Lucretia Mott (Courtesy of Friends Historical Library, Swarthmore College)

Cady Stanton's desires, a document she'd known by heart since childhood: The Declaration of Independence, the statement published to the world at the beginning of America's first revolution. At the end of that hard-won war, America's independence from England was achieved and liberty promised to those within its borders. But that visionary promise had yet to become a reality for any group other than white men; in many ways, the revolution remained incomplete and in need of a second stage. To usher in that stage, Cady Stanton and the others worked from the original declaration, substituting "all men" for "King George." They thought this was perfect. After all, they reasoned, the liberty women longed for was nothing more—and nothing less—than the liberty supposedly guaranteed to all Americans.

Cady Stanton began to draft the Declaration of Rights and Sentiments. Its opening words would be well-known: "When, in the course of human events, it becomes necessary for one portion of the family of man to assume among the people of the earth a position different from that which they have hitherto occupied, but one to which the laws of nature and of nature's God entitle them, a decent respect to the opinions of mankind requires that they should declare the causes that impel them to such a course." She repeated what she was sure were America's most beloved words: "We hold these truths to be self-evident." And then she decided to change history: "We hold these truths to be self-evident: that all men and women are created equal; that they are endowed by their Creator with certain inalienable rights; that among these are life, liberty, and the pursuit of happiness."

Mott went with her sister back to Auburn. Cady Stanton continued. "The history of mankind is a history of repeated injuries and usurpations on the part of man toward woman, having in direct object the establishment of an absolute tyranny over her."

As the date of the convention grew nearer, Cady Stanton worked with painstaking care to isolate woman's grievances: "He has compelled her to submit to laws, in the formation of which she had no voice. . . . He has taken from her all right in property, even to the wages she earns." She enumerated 18 in all, the same number of grievances listed in the Declaration of Independence. Then she fashioned resolutions to address these grievances.

Lucretia Mott, Mary Ann M'Clintock, her husband, Thomas M'Clintock, and others joined Cady Stanton for a final discussion. They enthusiastically endorsed the first eight resolutions. But her ninth resolution stated, "it is the duty of the women of this country to secure to themselves their sacred right to the elective franchise." Lucretia Mott expressed shock. Henry Stanton objected as well. Originally supportive of the convention, he threatened to leave town for its duration if his wife went so far as to demand woman suffrage. That, he said, would make a "farce" of an otherwise serious endeavor. But Elizabeth Cady

Stanton prevailed, and the resolution concerning woman suffrage was included. Then the last resolutions were added, and the document was complete.

On July 19, 1848, the women gathered outside the Wesleyan Chapel on Fall Street. The church, built in 1843, no longer exists, nor has a picture of it ever been located. It was most probably a white, wood frame building with a peaked roof and an unadorned steeple, much like other 19th century churches still dotting the countryside. The door was locked, but a window was open. Cady Stanton asked her small nephew to climb through and quickly unlock the door from inside. Well over a hundred people were coming down Fall Street.

As the people neared the chapel, Cady Stanton realized she and the other organizers had a problem: Many of those approaching were men. Gender-mixed groups were called "promiscuous" by the clergy and newspaper editors. The first abolitionist women to address such audiences were condemned from pulpit and headline alike. Although these women continued to speak, they were always careful to be introduced by a man—no woman had yet *led* a mixed meeting. Cady Stanton, Mott, and the others panicked. They almost agreed to eject the men from the meeting. Instead, they asked Lucretia Mott's husband, James Mott, to act as chairperson. He agreed, and the men were admitted and given full partici-pation in the convention.

When she was introduced, Cady Stanton read the Declaration of Rights and Sentiments from its first word to its last. Then a motion was passed to discuss the declaration one paragraph at a time. It was seriously debated for two days; some amendments were made as a result. But one by one, the resolutions were being adopted. They were resolutions Elizabeth Cady Stanton hoped would change the world. The first, "That such laws as conflict, in any way, with the true and substantial happiness of woman, are contrary to the great precept of nature, and of no validity," passed unanimously. The second, "That all laws which prevent woman from occupying such a station in her society as her conscience shall dictate, or which place her in a position inferior to that of man, are contrary to the great precept of nature, and therefore of no force or authority," was also passed, and also unanimously. And so forth and so on down the list of revolutionary demands until the ninth was reached.

Suddenly, there was no unanimous agreement. That women should vote was considered an almost unthinkable step. Cady Stanton pleaded with the crowd in the chapel, but to no avail. She was ready to accept defeat. At this moment, Frederick Douglass came to the front of the chapel and stood by her side. At her urgent prompting, her friend had come to take part in the convention. He began to speak, and the crowd grew quiet. Woman, like the slave, he said, had a right to liberty. He urged the women to understand just what the right of suffrage was, and why it was so crucial. "Suffrage," he said with powerful conviction, "is the power to choose rulers and make laws, and the right by which all others are secured."

After his speech, a majority passed the resolution. Reviewing his life a full 40 years later, Douglass would pick this moment as one of his best. "I have done very little in this world in which to glory except for this one act—and I certainly glory in that. When I ran away from slavery, it was for myself; when I advocated emancipation, it was for my people; but when I stood up for the rights of woman, self was out of the question, and I found a little nobility in the act."

The remaining resolutions were unanimously adopted, including the last, which Lucretia Mott had proposed. Mott wanted women to be able to become religious leaders, and her demand was "the overthrow of the monopoly of the pulpit"; to this she added a demand for women's "equal participation with men in the various trades, professions, and commerce."

It would be impossible to exaggerate the amount of scorn, ridicule, and hostility that greeted women after the convention. The event was reported in newspapers throughout the country. "They should have resolved at the same time that it was obligatory also upon the [men] to wash dishes, scour up, be put to the tub, handle the broom, darn stockings, patch breeches, scold the servants, dress in the latest fashion, wear trinkets, [and] look beautiful . . ." one newspaper declared, making fun of woman's sphere while consigning her to it. Others branded Cady Stanton, Mott, M'Clintock, Hunt, and Wright "sour old maids," "childless women," and "divorced wives," although they were none of these; the implications were that such "marginal" women could not speak for their sex. Underlying all the ridicule was the clear assumption that women were of value only insofar as they were of use (or of potential use) to men. As the *Philadelphia Public Ledger and Daily Transcript* explained, "A woman is nobody. A wife is everything. A pretty girl is equal to ten thousand men, and a mother is, next to God, all powerful. . . . The ladies of Philadelphia, therefore, . . . are resolved to maintain their rights as Wives, Belles, Virgins, and Mothers, and not as Women." In other words, a woman's "rights" were to be secured not by law, but by her ability to gain the indulgence of a fond, individual male.

There was private opposition as well. Henry Stanton, true to his word, left Seneca Falls during his wife's "farce," while his father-in-law, Judge Cady, rushed into town—to make sure his daughter hadn't gone insane. Other fathers, husbands, brothers, and sons applied such severe pressure that many of the original hundred signers—Cady Stanton's sister Harriet Eaton among them—later removed their names.

Cady Stanton wrote cheerful but uncompromising replies to each of her public opponents. She was perfectly satisfied with the controversy she'd caused. As she pointed out to the editor of Rochester's *National Reformer*, "There is no danger of this question dying for want of notice."

And indeed there was not. Within days of the Seneca Falls Convention, women in Rochester planned a convention of their own. When Mott and Cady Stanton arrived, they found progress: Not one of the Rochester organizers was willing to name a male president to address the "promiscuously" assembled audience.

The Rochester convention attracted a bride still "in travelling dress" who, with her husband, deliberately missed their train in order to attend the convention; it also attracted members of the clergy who'd been angered by reports from Seneca Falls. It was a loud and boisterous meeting. Abigail Bush, the woman leading the meeting, introduced speaker after speaker to answer objections to the Declaration of Rights and Sentiments. When it was finally adopted, Lucretia Mott walked over to Bush, who always remembered how the older woman "folded me tenderly in her arms and thanked me for presiding." So deeply did Bush feel her break with custom, that afterward, "my strength seemed to leave me and I cried like a baby."

At one point during the convention, the audience had demanded of chairperson Abigail Bush: "Louder, louder!"

"Friends," she'd answered, "we present ourselves here before you, as an oppressed class, with trembling frames and faltering tongues, and we do not expect to be able to speak so as to be heard by all at first . . ."

But they were heard—all across the country. By the end of 1850, women's rights conventions were held in the cities of Salem, Ohio, and Worcester, Massachusetts. People traveled from Maine, New York, New Hampshire, Vermont, Pennsylvania, Connecticut, Rhode Island, Iowa, Ohio, and California, and from all parts of Massachusetts, to attend the Worcester convention.

The Worcester convention was important for another reason, too: It marked the entrance of Lucy Stone into the organized women's movement.

Lucy Stone was born on August 13, 1818, on a farm just outside of West Brookfield, Massachusetts. She began to think about women's rights while still a young girl. Her parents, Francis Stone and Hannah Matthews Stone, had nine children, seven of whom survived. Seeing her mother's domestic burdens filled Lucy with anger and pity; from the time she was 12 years old, she woke early enough to do some of her mother's chores before leaving for school.

However, she would not share other burdens assigned to females. It was common for girls to join sewing circles. The garments they made were sold, and the monies received became contributions toward the tuition fees of young men studying to become ministers. (Since there was money involved, these sewing circles were required to have male treasurers.) Lucy Stone joined, but decided she couldn't finish the shirt she'd begun. "Let these men with broader shoulders and stronger arms earn their own education," she said, "while we use our scantier opportunities to educate ourselves." Though frequently going hungry in the process, she attended Oberlin College (founded in 1833, it was the first college open to women as well as men) and graduated with honors in 1847. She worked as a lecturer in the abolitionist movement, addressing threatening mobs and "promiscuous" audiences with a clear, sweet voice. Her equal concern for women was present from the start: "I expect to plead not for the slave only," she wrote to her mother, "but for suffering humanity everywhere. ESPECIALLY DO I MEAN TO LABOR FOR THE ELEVATION OF MY SEX." Helping to organize the Worcester, Massachusetts, women's rights convention in 1850, she embarked upon that work in earnest.

Cady Stanton, for her part, returned home from the Seneca Falls and Rochester conventions a much happier woman. She'd turned her personal despair to positive use and found it "a great relief." Moreover, she now found Seneca Falls to be a bit more stimulating than she had at first. As she reported to Lucretia Mott, "[M]y humble village is . . .made famous . . ." After the convention, Seneca Falls residents and reformers traveling through to Rochester or Syracuse began to seek out Elizabeth Cady Stanton. To a large extent, she and Henry were able to resume the stimulating social life they'd previously enjoyed in Boston.

Cady Stanton's feeling about her marriage changed as well. Having become what Lucretia Mott called the "pioneer," she was now much busier than before. But she was no longer overwhelmed. "With these new duties and interests," she explained, "and a broader outlook on human life, my petty domestic annoyances gradually took a subordinate place." Difficulties between Elizabeth and Henry were eased; their fourth son, Theodore, was born in 1851.

It was a time when few women mentioned their pregnancies in public. After the Seneca Falls Convention, however, Elizabeth Cady Stanton hoisted flags to the tops of flagpoles to announce her own safe deliveries of infants: a red flag for Theodore in 1851 and a triumphant white for her first daughter, Margaret, born in 1852. No one said, "What a pity it is she's a girl!" when Elizabeth brought forth her female child. Nor did anyone express pity for her in childbed: She viewed childbirth as a healthy exercise of female ability and sometimes stopped working only 15 minutes before a baby's arrival. When Theodore was born, she gloated to Henry: "I am regarded as a perfect wonder. Many people are actually impatiently waiting for me to die in order to make their theories good."

Henry was more supportive of his wife's beliefs and unconventional behavior than his deliberate absence from the Seneca Falls Convention might seem to indicate. In 1851 he demonstrated the strength of that support. In the winter of that year,

Cady Stanton's cousin Libby Smith discarded the customary clothing of the 19th-century female and appeared in an outfit of her own design. It featured a short skirt worn over "pantaloons" without corsets or other confining undergarments. When Seneca Falls resident Amelia Bloomer printed the pattern in her temperance newspaper, it became known as "the Bloomer," and then just "bloomers."

Clothing reform was not a frivolous side issue: Women were truly imprisoned in their clothing. Nineteenth-century corsets applied an average of 21 pounds of pressure to a woman's abdominal area, and some corsets applied as much as 88 pounds of pressure. The skirts that descended from this constricted center weighed, again on average, almost 20 pounds, and they dragged in layers on the ground. Many women were maimed. Prolapsed uteri, broken ribs, and damaged internal organs were common in the middle- and upper-class women who wore corsets. Both poor and wealthy women wore their dresses long, losing the use of one hand to the continual lifting of skirts. It's hard for people today to realize just how physically limiting this was, but Cady Stanton lived with it every day. And she knew an improvement when she saw it: "To see my cousin, with a lamp in one hand and a baby in the other, walk upstairs with ease and grace," she ruminated, "while, with flowing robes, I pulled myself up with difficulty, lamp and baby out of the question . . ." She immediately adopted bloomers.

Wherever she went, crowds gathered and stared. Judge Cady refused to allow her to visit "in shorts." Her sons didn't want their mother seen "in costume." But Henry found his very career threatened. He was running for elective office at the time, and Elizabeth's dress was used against him. During the campaign, voters repeatedly told him they wouldn't elect a man whose wife wore bloomers. On election day, people jeered in the streets:

> Heigh! ho! the carrion crow,
> Mrs. Stanton's all the go;
> Twenty tailors take the stitches,
> Mrs. Stanton wears the breeches.

Stanton nonetheless supported his wife's right to reform her attire. Her support for him was strong in return. He won his seat in the New York state Senate by a narrow margin. Even though his victory would take him from home for much of each year, she wholeheartedly congratulated him. To Libby Smith, she confided: "I would sooner see every relative and friend I have on the face of the earth blown into thin air . . . than have had Henry mortified by a defeat in this election."

As it turned out, she did not find herself without a companion in Seneca Falls. In 1851, while wearing her bloomers, she was introduced to Susan B. Anthony. "There she stood," Cady Stanton would later recall, "with her good, earnest face and genial smile . . . I liked her thoroughly, and why I did not at once invite her home with me to dinner, I do not know. She accuses me of that neglect, and has never forgiven me . . ." This was the inauspicious beginning of what was to become her very closest friendship and working partnership.

Susan B. Anthony was born on a farm outside of Adams, Massachusetts, on February 15, 1820. Her father was Daniel Anthony, a prosperous Quaker; her mother was Lucy Read

Susan B. Anthony (engraving by G.E. Perine & Co., New York, from Elizabeth Cady Stanton et al., *History of Woman Suffrage*, Vol. 1)

Anthony. Although the Anthonys were not practicing Quakers, their lives were guided by Quaker principles. These included, among other things, a firm belief in the equality of men and women. When the teacher in the local school refused to allow the bright but female Susan to progress beyond a certain point in math, her father founded a school in his own home.

When Susan was 17, Daniel Anthony lost most of his money. He nonetheless exhausted his few remaining funds to send his daughter to a female seminary. Although she was able to attend the seminary for only one term, she was afterward able to find work as a teacher. She worked very hard and helped to pay the debts her father had incurred. By the time she was 26, she was headmistress of the Female Department of the Canajoharie Academy, in Canajoharie, New York—a small town not far from Johnstown.

In 1848, Susan's mother, father, and sister Mary attended the women's rights convention in Rochester, New York. Although they reported the details to her, Susan was not immediately moved to action; her energies were already committed to the temperance and abolition movements, and to trying to improve the status of working women through participation in the New York State Teachers' Association. Eventually, though, she realized that it was difficult for a legally handicapped woman to have any impact upon her society.

She was visiting Amelia Bloomer in 1851 in connection with their mutual temperance work when she was introduced to Elizabeth Cady Stanton. Within a short time, Cady Stanton and Anthony became an indivisible unit, committed to the cause of women's rights. "In thought and sympathy we were one, and in the division of labor we exactly complemented each other," Cady Stanton said later. "In writing we did better work than either could alone. While she is slow and analytical in composition, I am rapid and synthetic. I am the better writer, she the better critic. She supplied the facts and statistics, I the philosophy and rhetoric, and, together, we have made arguments that have stood unshaken through the storms of long years; arguments that no one had answered."

It was Susan B. Anthony's friendship that enabled Elizabeth Cady Stanton to continue her chosen work while raising her children. When a speech was needed, Anthony came to Seneca Falls, where she "stirred the puddings" and disciplined her friend's youngsters. If Cady Stanton couldn't leave home to get the necessary facts, Anthony searched out and delivered them. Then, if Cady Stanton couldn't get to a given convention, Anthony took the speech and delivered that, too.

But what Cady Stanton most gratefully remembered was Anthony's refusal to see her friend swallowed by domesticity. "Mrs. Stanton," as Anthony always called her, loved her children; however, she sometimes felt completely overrun with them. Anthony always acknowledged the situation but at the same time urged her friend to transcend it. "So, for the love of me and for the saving of the reputation of womanhood, I beg you, with one baby on your knee and another at your feet, and four boys whistling, buzzing, hallowing 'Ma, Ma,' set yourself about the work . . . Ah! Mrs. Stanton, don't say No, nor don't delay it [the writing of a speech] a moment; for I must have it all done and almost commit[ted] to memory."

With Anthony, and with the help of Amelia Willard (no relation to Emma Willard), a young woman who became the family's housekeeper during this time, Cady Stanton launched an organized women's rights movement. Beginning in 1850, national conventions were held annually; Cady Stanton attended when she could and sent a speech when she couldn't. She was invited to speak before other audiences, too. Altogether, between 1848 and 1854, she delivered eight public addresses, published articles in Rochester's *National Reformer* and Amelia Bloomer's *The Lily*, wrote various newspaper editorials and public letters, and was elected president of the Woman's [New York] State Temperance Society.

But the highlight of this period, what Cady Stanton later called "a great event in my life," occurred in 1854. At a women's rights convention held in Rochester, New York, on November 30 and December 1, 1853, a committee including Elizabeth Cady Stanton, Susan B. Anthony, and Ernestine Rose was appointed to request a public audience with the New York state legislature. The committee also circulated a pair of petitions. The first petition requested an extension of the Married Women's Property Act; the second, a women's suffrage amendment to the state constitution. In 1836, Ernestine Rose had found only five women willing to sign her petition; now, a half-dozen years after the Seneca Falls Convention, 13,000 women and men signed their names. The legislature agreed to hear a representative of the new women's rights movement, and Elizabeth Cady Stanton became what her teacher, Emma Willard, had earlier wished to be: the first woman to address the New York state legislature.

She worked through many nights on her speech, trying to put everything she knew of women's position into convincing words. Then, with her papers, her three smallest children, and Amelia Willard, she set out for Albany—via Johnstown. Once again, she sat in her father's office. Just days before, a guest in the Cady home had written a letter describing Daniel Cady, now in his eighties, as "not a 'woman's rights' man." Elizabeth had every reason to know this was true; her father had disinherited her and cut her off without a cent at least once since the Seneca Falls Convention. But he was still "the one of all others whose approbation I most desired." She'd signed one of her recent letters to him, "Your affectionate but radical daughter," and was pleased he wanted to hear her speech.

Reading it, she "threw all the pathos I could into my voice and language . . . and, to my intense satisfaction, I saw tears filling my father's eyes. I cannot express the exultation I felt, thinking that now he would see, with my eyes, the injustice women suffered under the laws he knew so well."

When she finished speaking, he turned to her. What her father said, Cady Stanton recorded in her autobiography. "Surely you have had a happy, comfortable life, with all your wants and needs supplied; and yet that speech fills me with self-reproach; for one might naturally ask, how can a young woman, tenderly brought up, who has had no bitter personal experience, feel so keenly the wrongs of her sex? Where did you learn this lesson?"

"I learned it here, in your office, when a child," Elizabeth responded, "listening to the complaints women made to you. They who have sympathy and imagination to make the sorrow of others their own can readily learn all the hard lessons of life from the experience of others."

The two looked at each other for a long time. Finally, Judge Cady stood up. "Well," he said, "you have made your points clear and strong; but I think I can find you even more cruel laws than those you have quoted."

Judge Cady took several books from his shelf and turned to pages containing extremely harsh laws about women: laws that allowed the seizure of a wife's wages and property in order to settle her husband's debts, for example, and laws that permitted husbands to use physical force to punish their wives.

On February 14, 1854, Elizabeth Cady Stanton—once an angry little girl with a pair of scissors—stood as a self-possessed woman of 38 in the Senate chamber, speaking on behalf of women. "Yes, gentlemen, in republican America, in the nineteenth century," she began,

> we, the daughters of the revolutionary heroes of '76, demand at your hands the redress of our grievances—a revision of your State Constitution—a new code of laws. Permit us then, as briefly as possible, to call your attention to the legal disabilities under which we labor . . .
>
> We are persons; native, free-born citizens; property-holders, tax-payers; yet we are denied the exercise of our right to the elective franchise . . . True, the unmarried woman has a right to the property she inherits and the money she earns, but she is taxed without representation . . . [Since women are not allowed to serve on juries], among the hundreds of women who are shut up in prisons in this State, not one has enjoyed that most sacred of all rights—the right which you would die to defend for yourselves—trial by a jury of one's peers . . .
>
> The wife who inherits no property holds about the same legal position that does the slave on the Southern plantation. She can own nothing, sell nothing. She has no right even to the wages she earns; her person, her time, her services are the property of another. She can not testify, in many cases, against her husband . . . she can neither sue nor be sued. She is not held morally responsible for any crime committed in the presence of her husband, so completely is her very existence supposed by the law to be merged in another. Think of it; your wives may be libelers [and] burglars . . . and for crimes like these they are not held amenable to the laws of the land, if they but commit them in your dread presence . . .
>
> How could man ever look thus on woman? . . . By the common law of England, the spirit of which has been but too faithfully incorporated into our statute law, a husband has a right to whip his wife with a rod not larger than his thumb, to shut her up in a room, and administer whatever moderate chastisement he may deem necessary to insure obedience to his wishes . . .

It is impossible to make the Southern planter believe that his slave feels and reasons just as he does—that injustice and subjection are as galling as to him—that the degradation of living by the will of another, the mere dependent on his caprice, at the mercy of his passions, is as keenly felt by him as his master. If you can force on his unwilling vision a vivid picture of the Negro's wrongs, and for a moment touch his soul, his logic brings him instant consolation. He says, the slave does not feel this as I would. Here, gentlemen, is our difficulty: When we plead our cause before the law-makers . . . they cannot take in the idea that men and women are alike . . . You scorn the thought that she [woman] has any natural love of freedom burning in her breast, any clear perception of justice urging her on to demand her rights.

Would to God you could know the burning indignation that fills woman's soul when she turns over the pages of your statute books, and sees there how like feudal barons you freemen hold your women. Would that you could know the humiliation she feels for sex, when she thinks of all the beardless boys in your law offices, learning these ideas of one-sided justice—taking their first lessons in contempt for all womankind—being indoctrinated into the incapacities of their mothers, and the lordly, absolute rights of man over all women, children, and property, and to know that these are to be our future presidents, judges, husbands, and fathers . . .

In conclusion, then, let us say, in behalf of the women of this State, we ask for all that you have asked for yourselves in the progress of your development, since the *Mayflower* cast anchor beside Plymouth Rock; and simply on the ground that the rights of every human being are the same and identical.

6

NO CHILD'S PLAY: 1855–69

Neither Elizabeth Cady Stanton's speech nor the signatures of 13,000 petitioning women prompted a change in New York State's laws in 1854. Nonetheless, an organized women's movement was clearly underway in America. National conventions continued to be held every year (with the exception of 1857) and attracted many women eager to join the cause. At the Ninth National Convention, held in New York City on May 12, 1859, the main issue discussed was the need to eliminate the word *male* from the various states' constitutions.

The Constitution of the United States as written in 1787 did not limit its guarantees of rights to men; beginning, "WE THE PEOPLE of the United States," it went on to discuss the citizenship rights of its "People" and "Persons." The president, and only the president, was referred to as "he." Otherwise, no hint of gender appeared in the document. It was Section 4 of the Constitution that stated "The Times, Places and Manner of holding Elections for Senators and Representatives, shall be prescribed in each State by the Legislature thereof . . ." And it was in the state constitutions that the word *male* appeared, limiting the exercise of voting and other rights to men. Women wanting to exercise the rights set forth in their "Declaration of Rights and Sentiments" faced a daunting task: the changing of each and every state constitution.

Another committee was appointed. Elizabeth Cady Stanton, Susan B. Anthony, Ernestine Rose, and Wendell Phillips, who had not forgotten the prejudiced treatment of women at the World Anti-Slavery Convention, were among its members. On behalf of those attending the Ninth National Convention, they sent a memorial to the legislature of every state in America, demanding that "whenever you shall remodel the Constitution of the State in which you live, the word 'male' shall be expurgated."

For some state legislatures, this was the first written notice of women's demands. This was not the case in New York, however, and legislators there were already considering another expanded women's property bill. A petition was therefore circulated and sent to the New York state legislature in addition to the memorial. The petitioners asked that women be granted suffrage, increased property rights, and equal guardianship of their children.

The Judiciary Committee's chairperson, Anson Bingham, said he was prepared to recommend the bill's passage. But first he wanted women themselves to make, as Anthony relayed the message, "our strongest arguments . . . before the Committee, and he says Mrs. Stanton must come."

This invitation came at a particularly difficult time for Elizabeth Cady Stanton. Her second daughter, Harriot, was born on January 20, 1856. Her fifth son and seventh child, Robert, was born on March 14, 1859, when Elizabeth was 43 years old. Although Elizabeth ran her flags up the flagpole in what had become her customary celebration, she was now exhausted after each of these deliveries. She wrote a candid letter to her cousin Libby Smith Miller after Harriot's birth. "Oh, how my soul died within me, as I approached that dreadful, never-to-be-forgotten ordeal . . . The deed was done and here I am in the land of the living rejoicing that a female is born to the world." Robert's birth was no easier. "I have a great boy, now three weeks old," she wrote to Susan B. Anthony. "He weighed at his birth without a particle of clothing 12¼ pounds. I never suffered so much. I was sick all the time before he was born, and I have been very weak ever since. He seemed to take up every particle of my vitality, soul and body. Thank Heaven! I am through the siege once more." Late that year, she suffered the loss of her father: Daniel Cady died on October 31, at the age of 86.

Susan B. Anthony was worried that Cady Stanton might not go to Albany under the circumstances. She wrote to Martha Coffin Wright, "I write her [Cady Stanton] this mail, but I wish you would step over there and make her feel that the salvation of the Empire State, or at least the women in it, depends upon her bending all her powers to moving the hearts of our law-

Elizabeth Cady Stanton and her daughter Harriot, 1858 (Courtesy of Seneca Falls Historical Society)

makers at this time . . . Mrs. Stanton must move heaven and earth now to secure this bill, and she can, if she will only try." In return, Cady Stanton wrote to reassure Anthony. "I can not, my dear friend, 'move heaven and earth,' but I will do what I can with pen and brain."

On February 18, 1860, Elizabeth Cady Stanton stood once more before the New York state legislature. She called her speech "A Slave's Appeal"—referring not to African-Americans in bondage, but to American women of all racial and economic backgrounds:

> Allow me . . . to call the attention of that party now so much interested in the slave of the Carolinas, to the similarity in his condition and that of the mothers, wives, and daughters of the Empire State. The negro has no name. He is Cuffy Douglas or Cuffy Brooks, just whose Cuffy he may chance to be. The woman has no name. She is Mrs. Richard Roe or Mrs. John Doe, just whose Mrs. she may chance to be. Cuffy has no rights to his earnings; he can not buy or sell or lay up anything that he can call his own. Mrs. Roe has no right to her earnings; she can neither buy nor sell, make contracts, nor lay up anything that she can call her own. Cuffy has no right to his children; they can be sold from him at any time. Mrs. Roe has no right to her children; they may be bound out to cancel a father's debts . . . The unborn child, even by the last will of the father, may be placed under the guardianship of a stranger and a foreigner. Cuffy has no legal existence; he is subject to restraint and moderate chastisement. Mrs. Roe has no legal existence; she has not the best right to her own person [a reference to a woman's legal obligation to accede to her husband's sexual advances]. The husband has the power to restrain, and administer moderate chastisement.
>
> Blackstone declares that the husband and wife are one, and learned commentators have decided that that one is the husband . . .
>
> The prejudice against color, of which we hear so much, is no stronger than against sex. It is produced by the same cause, and manifested very much in the same way. The negro's skin and the woman's sex are both *prima facie* evidence that they were intended to be in subjection to the white Saxon man. The few social privileges which the man gives the woman, he makes up to the negro in civil rights. The woman may sit at the same table and eat with the white man; the free negro may own property and [in New York State] vote. The woman may sit in the same pew with the white man in church; the free negro may enter the pulpit and preach. Now, with the black man's right to suffrage, the right . . . to minister at the altar, it is evident that the prejudice against sex is more deeply rooted and more unreasonably maintained than

that against color. As citizens of a republic, what should we most highly prize, social privileges or civil rights? The latter, most certainly ...

Now do not think, gentlemen, we wish you to do a great many troublesome things for us ... We ask no more than ... 'Let us alone.' In mercy, let us take care of ourselves, our property, our children, and our homes ... There has been a great deal written and said about protection. We, as a class, are tired of one kind of protection, that which leaves us everything to do, to dare, to suffer, and strips us of all means of its accomplishment ... Undo what man did for us in the dark ages, and strike out all special legislation for us; strike the words 'white male' from all your constitutions, and then, with fair sailing, let us sink or swim, live or die, survive or perish together.

The bill under consideration—"An Act Concerning the Rights and Liabilities of Husband and Wife"—passed, greatly increasing the rights of married women in New York State. A married woman could now conduct business separately from her husband, make contracts, sue and be sued regarding her own property or business, and sue "for any injury to her person or character, the same as if she were sole" (a new acknowledgment that a married woman had a character and reputation separate from her husband's). Women were also declared joint guardians of their children. This was a great victory. It was also the last time Cady Stanton would be able, without causing rancor, to reiterate her understanding of how closely the situation of women resembled that of the slave.

While the women's movement has been consolidating and gathering its strength, the United States had come to the brink of civil war. During the presidential campaign of 1860, Abraham Lincoln's Republican party adopted as part of its platform an antislavery plank forbidding the further spread of slavery in the United States. Spokesmen for Southern slaveholdng states issued a warning: If Lincoln became president, they would secede. The day after Abraham Lincoln was elected to that office, a confederate flag was flown in Charleston. Within the next two weeks, South Carolina's legislature scheduled a convention to discuss succession, and both South Carolina and Georgia began raising armies. When South Carolina, Mississippi, Florida and Alabama seceded, Northerners opposed to slavery responded. Lucretia Mott, Martha Coffin Wright, Gerrit Smith, Frederick Douglass, Susan B. Anthony, and Elizabeth Cady Stanton traveled throughout New York State in January of 1861, speaking against slavery.

Rioting resulted. Many Northerners held abolitionists responsible for the secession of Southern states and for the war they correctly believed was coming. During what she'd later call "the winter of mobs," Anthony was burned in effigy. She and Cady Stanton were the targets of rotten eggs, shouted insults, and pointed pistols. When they reached Buffalo, police officers sided with the mob and refused to break it up, despite orders from the mayor.

Cady Stanton had not faced such danger before. Henry Stanton had, and he wrote hurriedly to his wife: "In the present temper of the public mind, it is of no use to try to hold Abolition meetings in large cities. I think you risk your lives . . . [T]he mobcats would as soon kill you as not." She returned home to reassure him but left after a brief stay. She quickly caught up with Anthony in Albany. When a riot broke out, Mayor Thatcher pledged to protect both Cady Stanton and Anthony; that night, he attended their meeting with a gun.

When the Civil War began in the spring of 1861, Cady Stanton gave her enthusiastic support to the North. Writing to Secretary of State William Henry Seward to ask for a recommendation for her son Henry, who wished to enter West Point, she said, "The age of bullets has come again; and a rotten aristocracy [the South] must be subdued by the only weapons they can feel. I have an unwavering faith in the endurance of the Republic . . . This war is music in my ears." Her sons agreed. The youngest boys conducted mock drills about the house. Henry B. Stanton, Jr., just 17 years old, did not wait for Secretary Seward's reply; instead, he ran away to join the Union Army.

Susan B. Anthony, however, objected to the war and to her friend's enthusiasm. It was a war to preserve the Union, she pointed out, and not a war to end slavery. President Lincoln was clear about this in the spring of 1861: "I have no purpose, directly or indirectly, to interfere with slavery in the States where it exists." Moreover, Anthony realized, the war threatened to delay the emancipation of women. Their 10th national convention had been held in February, and another was scheduled for May. As soon as the first guns were fired, though, women began to insist that the May convention—and all subsequent public meetings—be canceled. Martha Coffin Wright spoke for many of the activists, saying "when the nation's whole heart and soul are engrossed with this momentous crisis . . . nobody will listen."

Wright's instincts were correct. On April 17, 1861, just days after Fort Sumter was attacked, the Soldier's Aid Society was formed by women in Cleveland, Ohio. Soldiers were about to be wounded, and these women wanted to be prepared to care for them. Similar societies were formed in cities throughout the North; on April 29th, they merged into the Women's Central Association of Relief, with headquarters in New York City.

Even Anthony had to admit that women's energies were about to be spent in the war. Reluctantly, she agreed to suspend the women's rights movement. "I am sick at heart," she wrote to one woman, "but I cannot carry the world against the wish and will of our best friends."

Cady Stanton suffered no such anguish over the decision. Unlike Anthony (and despite the mobs she'd encountered), she believed that popular Northern opinion would turn this into a war that would, after all, free the slaves. And she thought Northern women, working with Northern men toward a Union victory, would prove their worth as full and equal citizens.

Not even Elizabeth Cady Stanton, however, could have predicted the full scope of women's response to the war. In May, members of the Women's Central Association of Relief and two medical associations met with the secretary of War. They told the secretary that women were ready to receive nurse's training and to serve the troops. President Lincoln approved, and the United States Sanitary Commission was formed on June 13, 1861.

Its nurses rode horseback into battle, staffed hospital ships, and set up tents in the midst of soldiers' camps, all in an effort to provide immediate medical attention to the wounded. The supplies they needed were sent, not by the government, but by the women who remained behind. These women, holding fairs and bake sales, and asking for contributions, managed to raise an amazing $500,000,000 "for the benefit of the soldier." Women made shirts (one thousand a day in Boston), as well as blankets, socks, and bandages. When the battle of Antietam ended, leaving 17,000 wounded soldiers among 6,000 dead,

Leaving the Hospital for the Battlefield (engraved by G. E. Perine & Co., New York, from Frank Moore, *Women of the War*)

Sanitary Commission nurses were able to distribute "28,763 pieces of dry goods, shirts, towels, bed-ticks, pillows, etc.; 30 barrels of old linen, bandages, and lint; 3,188 pounds of farina; 2,620 pounds of condensed milk; 5,000 pounds of beef-stock and canned meats; 3,000 bottles of wine and cordials; 4,000 sets of hospital clothing; several tons of lemons and other fruit; crackers, tea, sugar, rubber cloth, tin cups, chloroform, opiates, surgical instruments, and other hospital conveniences."

Such efforts were well rewarded. In earlier wars, four soldiers died from illness or disease for every one soldier killed in battle or as a result of wounds. The Sanitary Commission reduced that ratio to two to one during the Civil War and thus saved 180,000 lives.

Women supported the war effort in other ways as well. Doctors examining dead and wounded soldiers found 400 of them to be women disguised as men. One, named Emily, wrote to her father after the battle of Chickamauga, September 19, 1863: "Forgive your dying daughter. I have but a few moments to live. My native soil drinks my blood. I expected to deliver my country, but the Fates would not have it so. I am content to die. Pray, pa, forgive me."

Harriet Tubman was another of the many women who rendered remarkable service. A fugitive slave, she'd made about 19 trips back to the South to rescue her elderly parents and other enslaved people. When the Civil War began, she offered her help to the Union army. She worked as a nurse, a spy, and a scout. Her assistance was applauded on the front page of the *Boston Commonwealth*, July 10, 1863: "Col. Montgomery and his gallant band of 800 black soldiers, under the guidance of a black woman, dashed into the enemies' country, struck a bold and effective blow ... [and] brought off near 800 slaves and thousands of dollars worth of property, without losing a man or receiving a scratch!"

Cady Stanton's belief that women would prove valuable allies seemed to be confirmed. But Susan B. Anthony's despair upon suspending the women's movement had also been well founded. In 1862, as the war progressed and ever-increasing numbers of New York women were widowed, the state legislature rescinded the major portions of the Married Women's Property Act of 1860. Equal custody of children was no longer a mother's right, and a widow was no longer awarded control of a husband's estate for use in raising whatever children were left in her care. "Well, well," Anthony wrote to her friend Lydia

Midnight on the Battlefield (engraved by J. J. Cade, New York; published by A. D. Worthington & Co. Publishers, Hartford, Conn., 1887. From Mary A. Livermore, *My Story of the War*)

Mott, "while the old guard sleep the young 'devils' are wide-awake, and we deserve to suffer for our confidence in 'man's sense of justice,' and to have all we have gained thus snatched from us."

Nevertheless, during the second half of the war, Susan B. Anthony joined forces with Elizabeth Cady Stanton to unite Northern women. The Emancipation Proclamation, issued January 1, 1863, freed slaves only in the rebel states. When the Thirteenth Amendment, freeing all the slaves, was introduced, Cady Stanton and Anthony formed the National Woman's Loyal League to petition in its favor. They were joined by 12-year-old Theodore Stanton and two thousand women, including Ernestine Rose, Angelina Grimké Weld, Martha Coffin Wright, Lucy Stone (by now married to abolitionist Henry B. Blackwell and famous for keeping her own surname), and the Rev. Antoinette B. Blackwell (Lucy Stone's sister-in-law and first American woman to become a minister outside the Quaker faith). They collected and rolled 400,000 petitions in favor of the amendment, many more than the young Senate pages could lift. Two free African-American adults carried the first installment into the Senate chamber and dropped it on the desk of Senator Charles Sumner. Sumner had introduced the amendment. Now, pointing to the petitions, he said he had proof than many thousands of people supported it.

White southern women worked every bit as hard as their Northern sisters. They turned their homes and churches into hospitals. They ran blockades; that is, they managed to cross enemy lines to get food and clothing for their families. A number were daring spies. But when Cady Stanton referred afterward to "the grand women who did faithful service in the late war," she was not referring to these women. "They," she wrote in 1863, "appreciate the blessings of slavery . . . " and live as "aristocrats with a lower class . . . entrenched in feudal homes . . . [where] babies [are] sold by the pound, and beautiful women sold for the vilest purposes of lust . . ." They were also participants in a rebellion against what Cady Stanton believed was "the grandest nation on the globe." She had based her own "Declaration of Rights and Sentiments" on the American "Declaration of Independence" and had introduced herself to the New York state legislature as one of "the daughters of the revolutionary heroes of '76." In her view, the freedoms she demanded for women were particularly American ones. And so, while she specifically demanded equality and suffrage for black women who'd been enslaved in the South and while she admired and later praised Southern women who, like abolitionist Angelina Grimké, took the Union side, she felt no sisterhood for Southern secessionist women during the Civil War.

The war finally ended in the spring of 1865. At the end of the year, on December 18, the Thirteenth Amendment was ratified and slavery abolished forever in all the United States. Cady Stanton had hoped for an end to slavery as one result of the war, and she celebrated that outcome. But she had also hoped that the efforts of "loyal women" would prompt legislators to grant what had been demanded since the Seneca Falls Convention in 1848: an acknowledgment of women's right to full, voting citizenship. To her anguish, it became clear that this was not going to happen.

The Thirteenth Amendment consisted of 43 words—43 words intended to correct a situation of several hundred years' standing, a situation that had, thus far, been sanctioned by the Constitution and upheld by the Supreme Court. Only seven years prior, in 1857, that Court had ruled against Dred Scott, a slave suing for his freedom. The question, the Court acknowledged, was simple: "Can a negro, whose ancestors were imported into this country, and sold as slaves, become a member of the political community formed and brought into existence by the Constitution of the United States, and as such become entitled to all the rights, and privileges, and immunities, guaranteed by that instrument to the citizen?" To find an answer, the justices consulted "the legislation and histories of the times, and the language used in the Declaration of Independence." It was clear, the Court decided, that "neither the class of persons who has been imported as slaves, *nor their descendants, whether they had become free or not,*" [emphasis added] were citizens. And Dred Scott, who was, according to the decision, "not a citizen . . . within the meaning of the Constitution of the United States," was not even "entitled . . . to sue in its courts."

Therefore, in the summer of 1865, right after the Civil War's end and even before the Thirteenth Amendment was finally ratified, Northern legislators (who constituted the entire Congress at this point, since the defeated Confederate states were not yet re-admitted into the Union) began to consider how to extend not just freedom, but citizenship, to African-Americans. One legislator, sympathetic to the women's movement, sent a draft to Elizabeth Cady Stanton and Susan B. Anthony. It proposed an amendment to the Constitution penalizing states that denied suffrage to any of their male inhabitants. While this would encourage states to extend suffrage to African-American males, it would also pointedly exclude women—and, for the first time, introduce the word *male* into the Constitution of the United States.

Cady Stanton contacted the abolitionists with whom she'd worked, to ask for clarification of their positions. Wendell Phillips wrote to her on May 10, 1865. "I am now engaged in abolishing slavery in a land where abolition of slavery means conferring or recognizing citizenship," he explained, "and where citizenship supposes the ballot for all men." Cady Stanton asked in return, "Do you believe the African race is composed entirely of males?" This was no rhetorical question. The women Cady Stanton referred to faced a struggle every bit as hard as that faced by men.

When slavery ended, many black women stayed on their former owner's property; they received wages for their work, paid rent for their shelter and made little or no profit. As one woman put it, "Didn't many of us go, 'cause we didn't know where to of went." Although these women and their children were no longer slaves, many a former master found the change impossible to comprehend. The Freedmen's Bureau, an agency created to help the former slaves, was flooded with women's complaints in the years following the war. Rhody Ann Hope charged that her former owner and current employer, Samuel Davison "beat her with fist and with the trace of an artillery harness. Alledged cause: Daughter of freedwoman was not there at dinner time to keep the flies off the table." Angeline Hollins' charge against James Lea was similar: "Complaints are made that you abused her very severely because she would not let her child go to the field to work before breakfast."

Slave women had suffered sexually as well as for reasons of race, as Cady Stanton had first learned during her teenage encounter with the fleeing Harriet. When slavery ended, rape and other forms of sexual abuse continued. Sickening accounts of what one Alabama doctor called "splitting a nigger woman," occur frequently in the Freedmen's Bureau records.

Cady Stanton "argued constantly with Phillips and the whole fraternity," as she wrote to Anthony, trying to convince them to support suffrage for black men and all women. Writing again to Phillips, she cited not the life women had endured in slavery, but the future they could expect to share with America's disenfranchised white women: "You say 'This is the negro's hour' . . . Again, if the two millions of southern black women are not to be secured in their rights of person, property, wages, and children, then their emancipation is but another form of slavery . . . We who know what absolute power is given to man, in all his civil, political, and social relations, by the statute laws of most of the states, demand that in changing the status of four millions of Africans, the women as well as the men shall be secured in all the rights, privileges, and immunities of citizens." Moreover, she was afraid that black men, for whom she wrote in the same letter, "the representative women of the nation have done their uttermost to secure freedom," would not return the favor. "Is there not danger that he, once entrenched in all his inalienable rights, may be an added power to hold us at bay? Why should the African prove more just and generous than his Saxon compeers?"

Many of the male abolitionists had endorsed women's suffrage before and, like Phillips and Douglass, had taken part in women's rights conventions. All of the women's rights leaders had worked to end slavery. But now the male leaders of the abolitionist movement refused to "mix the movements," as Phillips put it. Cady Stanton wrote to Anthony, who was visiting her brother in Kansas, "I fear one and all will favor enfranchising the negro without us. Woman's cause is in deep water . . . Come back and help. There will be a room for you. I seem to stand alone."

On her way to New York City, where Elizabeth Cady Stanton now lived, Anthony stopped in Auburn, New York, to see Martha Coffin Wright. Wright was doubtful that the women's movement could be quickly resurrected in the face of abolitionist opposition, and she told Anthony so. But Anthony and Cady Stanton were determined to try. The two women talked all through the night of Anthony's arrival at Cady Stanton's home. Then, the next morning, Anthony left for a round of visits. She met with Mary Grew, Sarah Pugh, and James and Lucretia Mott in Philadelphia. She saw Lucy Stone and Antoinette Blackwell in New Jersey, and called on Abbey Kelley Foster in Worcester, Massachusetts. Everywhere she went, she asked for help in petitioning Congress for "an amendment of the Constitution that shall prohibit the several States from disfranchising any of their citizens on the ground of sex." Elizabeth Cady Stanton, meanwhile, wrote hundreds of letters to women all around the country, explaining the proposed addition of the word *male* and asking for signatures on the opposing petition.

When neither woman found immediate, wholehearted support, Cady Stanton began to write follow-up letters. "With . . . bills before Congress to exclude us from all hope of representation in the future by so amending the United States Constitution as to limit suffrage to 'males,'" she wrote furiously to Martha Coffin Wright, "I thank God *two* women of the nation felt the insult and decided to do their uttermost to rouse the rest to avail themselves of the only right we have left in the government—the right of petition. If the petition goes with two names only, ours be the glory, and shame to all the rest . . . if they come back to us empty, Susan and I will sign every one . . ."

To her relief she saw, as she said, "the skies begin to clear." Lucy Stone joined Cady Stanton and Anthony in signing a letter stating that "Propositions already have been made on the floor of Congress to amend the Constitution as to exclude women from a voice in the government. As this would be to turn the wheels of legislation backward, let the women of the nation now unitedly protest . . . and petition for . . . the right of representation." They collected 10,000 signatures.

In December of 1865, they also received an overture from one of the abolitionist men. Theodore Tilton, editor of the *New York Independent*, suggested a new organization, the American Equal Rights Association (AERA), and a merger of female and black male suffrage supporters.

Cady Stanton and Anthony scheduled the Eleventh National Women's Rights Convention for May of 1866 and placed Tilton's suggestion on the agenda. At the convention, women's rights activists voted to disband their own organization and join the AERA, whose stated goal was to "secure Equal Rights to all American citizens, especially the right of suffrage, irrespective of race, color, or sex." Supporters of suffrage for black men and all women would now, Cady Stanton thought, join their forces without reservation. She herself wrote the preamble for the new organization's constitution. In it, she declared, "we, today . . . bury the woman in the citizen, and our organization in the American Equal Rights Association." Lucretia Mott was elected president; Elizabeth Cady Stanton, first vice president, and Susan B. Anthony, one of three corresponding secretaries. Eleven others, in addition to Cady Stanton and Anthony, composed the Executive Committee. One of the 11 was Wendell Phillips.

Cady Stanton and Anthony expected a true coalition, but they were quickly disappointed. Twenty-one days later, the executive committee of the AERA met again—in Boston and without Elizabeth Cady Stanton or Lucretia Mott. And Wendell Phillips made his priorities clear: "the negro's . . . claim to this right [of suffrage] might fairly be considered to have precedence . . . This hour, then, is preeminently the property of the negro."

The Fourteenth Amendment was passed by Congress on June 13, 1866. Its first section declared that "All persons born or naturalized in the United States are citizens of the United States and of the State wherein they reside"—a revolutionary step forward from the *Dred Scott* decision of 1857. The second section, however, was what Cady Stanton had feared. It reduced the congressional representation of any state where "the right to vote . . . is denied to any of the male inhabitants."

That autumn, on October 10, 1866, Elizabeth Cady Stanton declared herself the first woman candidate for Congress. Although women were disfranchised, there was, according to her reading of the as yet gender-free Constitution, no barrier to their holding office. In her letter to the electors of the Eighth Congressional District, she declared, "as an Independent Candidate, I desire an election at this time, as a rebuke to the dominant party for its retrogressive legislation in so amending the National Constitution as to make invidious distinctions on the ground of sex." She was not challenged as to her right to run for office but received only 24 votes.

After this, she turned her attention to two state constitutions. In January of 1867, the New York state legislature called a Constitutional Convention. Cady Stanton addressed the Senate's Judiciary Committee on January 23 and insisted that women, as citizens governed by the state Constitution, had a right to vote for delegates empowered to change that document. Nine members agreed with her, but the motion, introduced by the Hon. Charles Folger, was defeated. She then asked for, and received, permission for women to address the convention when it convened the following summer. She, Susan B. Anthony, and Lucy Stone planned to speak, and a petition drive was immediately begun. Twenty thousand New York state women, including Margaret Livingston Cady, signed a petition demanding woman suffrage. Susan B. Anthony and Elizabeth Cady Stanton addressed the Constitutional Convention's suffrage subcommittee on June 27. Lucy Stone spoke on July 10. All three women asked, on behalf of themselves and the 20,000 petitioners, that women's suffrage be added to the Constitution.

Horace Greeley, the influential editor of the *New York Tribune*, was chairperson of that subcommittee. Despite his own wife's submission of a petition in favor of woman suffrage, he was "satisfied that public sentiment does not demand and would not sustain an innovation so revolutionary and sweeping . . ." Cady Stanton was disappointed in the report, but overjoyed that the press noticed Mary Greeley's plea.

Horace Greeley was not. At a party the following September, he and Cady Stanton had an unpleasant conversation, which Cady Stanton recounted in a letter to her friend Emily Holand. " . . .I have given," Greeley said angrily, "strict orders that you and your cause are to be tabooed in the future, and if it is necessary to mention your name, you will be referred to as 'Mrs. Henry B. Stanton.'"

"Mrs. Henry B. Stanton," not easily chastened, left for Kansas. Earlier that year, the Kansas legislature had decided to let the state's voters enfranchise women, black males, or both, on election day. Cady Stanton traveled there with Anthony in September of 1867. She had sometimes envied the occupants of "long, white-covered wagons, bound for the far West." Now, 51 years old, a bit heavier than in her youth but still vigorous and strong, she led the life of a pioneer for three months. She forded streams, crossed roadless prairies, and slept in beds provided by sympathetic strangers. She spoke about woman suffrage "wherever two dozen voters could be assembled . . . in log cabins, in depots, unfinished schoolhouses, churches, hotels, barns, and in the open air."

The Kansas campaign was exciting, but it was also the beginning of a severe breach between the women's rights leaders. Arriving in September of 1867, Cady Stanton and Anthony found that Republicans, heretofore the major party most in favor of women's suffrage, had formed an Anti-Female Suffrage Committee. There was virtually no chance that women's suffrage would be added to the state Constitution of Kansas.

Much later in her life, after her 78th birthday, Elizabeth Cady Stanton would accept a bitter reality: American women would not vote in her lifetime. Then she would write in her diary, "we are sowing winter wheat, which the coming spring will see sprout and which hands other than ours will reap and enjoy."

But she had not come to this acceptance yet; now she responded with rage and resentment. She attacked the black men she correctly believed would win suffrage before her and the white male abolitionists who refused to support the same access to power for women. African-American males, she said, "slaves, ignorant, degraded, depraved, but yesterday crouching at your [white male] feet, outside the pale of political consideration, are to-day, by your edicts, made her [woman's] lawgivers!" Her attacks on "Sambo," as she now sometimes referred to black males, continued after the ratification of the Fourteenth Amendment in July of 1868. In February of 1869, the Fifteenth Amendment was proposed. When this amendment— forbidding the denial of voting rights "on account of race, color, or previous condition of servitude"—did not include protection for sex, Cady Stanton's attacks escalated. Her former colleagues were appalled.

In Washington, a Joint Resolution was introduced on March 15, 1869. It suggested a 16th amendment forbidding disenfranchisement because of sex. Cady Stanton felt an "added dignity" and hoped the proposed amendment would serve as a "rallying point" for the now-divided reformers, but it did not. The final break came in May of 1869.

At an anniversary meeting of the American Equal Rights Association, Elizabeth Cady Stanton and Susan B. Anthony were criticized for an article that appeared in the *Revolution*, a newspaper they were then publishing. The article was titled "That Infamous Fifteenth Amendment" and its publication, Stephen Foster declared, "repudiated the principles of the [AERA] society." The meeting quickly became an examination of Cady Stanton's and Anthony's views on black male vs. female suffrage.

Anthony said that she refused to support the Fifteenth Amendment because "it did not mean equal rights; it put 2,000,000 colored men in the position of tyrants over 2,000,000 colored women, who until now had been at least the equals of the men at their side."

Frederick Douglass had come, and he was one of the first to answer Anthony. "I must say I do not see how anyone can pretend that there is the same urgency in giving the ballot to woman as to the negro," he said. "With us, the matter is a question of life and death, at least in fifteen States of the Union. When women, because they are women, are hunted down through the cities of New York and New Orleans; when they are dragged from their houses and hung upon lamp-posts; when their children are torn from their arms, and their brains dashed out upon the pavement; when they are objects of insult and outrage at every turn; when they are in danger of having their homes burnt down over their heads; when their children are not allowed to enter schools; then they will have an urgency to obtain the ballot equal to our own."

Someone from the audience called out, "Is that not true about black women?"

And Douglass answered, "Yes, yes, yes; it is true about the black woman, but not because she is a woman, but because she is black . . . Woman! why she has 10,000 modes of grappling with her difficulties."

Susan B. Anthony responded. " . . . When Mr. Douglass mentioned the black man first and the woman last, if he had noticed he would have seen that it was the men that clapped and not the women. There is not the woman born who desires to eat the bread of dependence, no matter whether it be from the hand of father, husband, or brother; for any one who does so eat her bread places herself in the power of the person from whom she takes it. Mr. Douglass talks about the wrongs of the negro; but with all the outrages that he to-day suffers, he would not exchange his sex and take the place of Elizabeth Cady Stanton."

Douglass then asked "whether the granting to woman the right of suffrage will change anything in respect to the nature of our sexes."

Angry, Anthony shot back: "It will change the nature of one thing very much, and that is the dependent condition of woman. It will place her where she can earn her own bread, so that she may go out into the world an equal competitor in the struggle for life; so that she shall not be compelled to take such positions as men choose to accord and then take such pay as men please to give . . . It is not a question of precedence between women and black men; the business of this association is to demand for every man, black or white, and every woman, black or white, that they shall be enfranchised and admitted into the body politic with equal rights and privileges."

A little later in the meeting, when the question of "free love" (sexual relations outside marriage) was raised, Anthony responded in carefully chosen words. "This howl [of free love] comes from the men who know that when women get their rights they will be able to live honestly and not be compelled to sell themselves for bread, either in or out of marriage." In her view, woman—without property rights, political power, or control of her own body after marriage—was being left, not with "10,000 modes of grappling with her difficulties," but one.

Lucy Stone added her opinion to Anthony's, telling Douglass that "woman suffrage is more imperative than his own; and I want to remind the audience that when he says what the Ku-Kluxes did all over the South, the Ku-Kluxes here in the North in the shape of men, take away children from the mother, and separate them just as completely as if done on the block of the auctioneer. Over in New Jersey they have a law which says that *any* father—he might be the most brutal man that ever existed—*any* father, it says, whether he be under age or not, may by his last will and testament dispose of the custody of his child, born or not born, and that such disposition shall be good against all persons, and that the mother shall not recover her child; and that law modified in form exists over every state in the Union except in Kansas. Woman has an ocean of wrongs too deep for any plummet," she continued, "and the negro, too, has an ocean of wrongs that cannot be fathomed. There are two great oceans; in the one is the black man, and in the other is the woman. But I thank God for that XV. Amendment and hope that it will be adopted in every State. I will be thankful in my soul if *any* body can get out of the terrible pit."

Cady Stanton and Anthony did not share Lucy Stone's concluding sentiments. Following this meeting, they founded the National Woman Suffrage Association (NWSA) to fight exclusively for women's rights and, especially, for women's suffrage.

It was not an organization that Lucy Stone wished to join. Near the end of 1869, she wrote to her former colleague, Elizabeth Cady Stanton: "I wish I could have had a quiet hour with you, to talk about it. I *hope* you will see it as I do . . . People will differ, as to what they consider the best methods and means. The true wisdom is not to ignore, but to provide for the fact. So far as I have influence, this soc.[iety] shall never be an

Lucy Stone (engraving from Elizabeth Cady Stanton et al., *History of Woman Suffrage*, Vol. 2)

enemy or antagonist of yours in any way . . . Your little girls, and mine will reap the easy harvest which it costs so much to sow." Stone was founding an alternate organization, the American Woman Suffrage Association.

Despite the wish expressed in Stone's letter, the two organizations quickly became rivals and took different routes to suffrage. Stone's American Woman Suffrage Association focused on obtaining an amendment to each of the state constitutions. Cady Stanton and Anthony's National American Woman Suffrage Association focused on obtaining the amendment to the United States Constitution.

As time went on, Stone and Cady Stanton disagreed over more than the Fifteenth Amendment. As first president of NWSA and editor of the *Revolution*, Cady Stanton discussed women's liberty in terms that frightened many. Although she believed in the value of romantic love, she refused to view the institution of marriage romantically. Instead, she examined the many ways in which marriage robbed women of their autonomy and even of their selfhood. Stone was not the only one shocked when Cady Stanton told an audience of 3,000 people, "I rejoice over every slave [every married woman] that escapes from a discordant marriage. With the education and elevation of woman we shall have a mighty sundering of unholy ties that hold men and women together who loathe and despise each other." When she was accused of being a supporter of free love, she answered the charge privately, in a letter to Libby Smith Miller: "You ask if I believe in free love.' If by 'free love' you mean woman's right to give her body to the man she loves and no other, to become a mother or not as her desire, judgment and conscience may dictate, to be the absolute sovereign of herself, then I do believe in freedom of love. The next step of civilization will bring woman to this freedom." Cady Stanton also insisted that women's sexual needs were equal to those of men; objected to religious teachings about women's place in society; and declared that female jurors should decide the fate of a woman charged with killing her newborn. Lucy Stone and her supporters thought statements such as these endangered the suffrage cause.

Cady Stanton was sorry to lose support, but she would not ask for less than what she really wanted for woman: Her liberty, broadly defined. As she said to Anthony, "The establishing of woman on her rightful throne is the greatest revolution the world has ever known or will know. To bring it about is no child's play . . . A journal called the *Rosebud* might answer for those who come with kid gloves and perfumes . . . but for us . . . there is no name like the *Revolution*."

7

THE SOLITUDE OF SELF: 1870–92

Elizabeth Cady Stanton and Susan B. Anthony were forced by their finances to sell the *Revolution* in 1870, and Cady Stanton took herself and her cause directly to the people. She joined a lecture circuit and traveled, as she had across Kansas, to speak to small groups about women's rights. For each of the next 10 years, she left her home, which was now a rambling house in Tenafly, New Jersey, as soon as the children started school in September. She traveled from September to Christmas, and from mid-January until the beginning of her children's summer vacation. Robert, her youngest child, was 10 when this began. She herself was 54. Her curls had whitened and she looked, according to one man, like "the mother of a governor or a president." But there was nothing staid about her.

In Delaware, Iowa, California—and most states and territories in between—she spoke to mixed audiences about women's suffrage. Then, in individual homes, she spoke with women alone about the very private concerns she had come to see as political: sexuality, marriage, birth control, maternity, and religion.

Elizabeth and Henry had become accustomed to living together for only a few months each year. The adjustment was much more difficult for the children. Harriot Stanton, who would herself be a feminist leader when grown, was just entering her teens at the time. In her autobiography, she recalled

> many memories of separation from my mother. Her going away was always an acute pain to me. I still attach to the whistle of an engine heard in the distance, the thought,

'mother is going away.' I do not remember her coming back, but she . . . told in later years how differently Margaret and I reacted. My sister gave her one enthusiastic embrace, and then skipped in circles around the family group, while I very slowly and shyly edged toward her, slipped into her lap, buried my face in her bosom, and wept as if my heart would break.

Elizabeth's mother and sisters willingly helped with childcare, but even this kind of assistance didn't guarantee regular correspondence. Once, too harried during a trip to write separate letters to her sisters, Elizabeth finally wrote one to be shared among "Dear Sisters, 1, 2, and 3." More seriously, Elizabeth was in California when she learned that Margaret Cady was severely ill. Although she rushed to Johnstown, she arrived only days before her mother's death in 1871.

Cady Stanton believed the woman's cause was worth extraordinary sacrifice. As she wrote to her daughter Margaret, " . . . above all considerations of loneliness and fatigue, I feel that I am doing an immense amount of good in rousing women to thought and inspiring them with new hope and self-respect, that I am making the path smoother for you and Hattie and all the other dear girls."

She did have reason to think that the path was indeed becoming smoother. In 1870, to her great delight, women in the territories of Wyoming and Utah were granted suffrage. (Although Utah's women would lose that right in 1887, the women of Wyoming would manage to keep it even after their territory's admission as the 44th state in 1890.) Almost immediately, women in Wyoming began to serve as jurors and one, Esther Morris, was appointed justice of the peace. There were advances in other states, too. All across the United States, women now went to college, became doctors, and were ordained as ministers.

Not all the news was good, though. In 1869, the year after the ratification of the Fourteenth Amendment, an attorney in Missouri had tried to point out what he saw as the applicability of the amendment to women. Francis Minor was the husband of Virginia Minor, president of the Woman Suffrage Association of Missouri. At a convention of the association, Minor directed women's attention away from the Fourteenth

Amendment's introduction of the word *male*, and to the amendment's first section, which explicitly extended citizenship to "all persons born and naturalized in the United States" and decreed that "No State shall make or enforce any law which shall abridge the privileges or immunities of citizens . . ." If these provisions could be shown to apply to women, Minor thought the Fourteenth Amendment could be viewed not as a step backward but as a step forward for women. He drew up resolutions stating that women, as citizens under the Fourteenth Amendment, could not have their "privileges," including suffrage, abridged by any state and that they were therefore entitled under the United States Constitution to vote. These resolutions were enthusiastically adopted at the convention.

Cady Stanton, deeply entrenched at the time in her opposition to the Fifteenth Amendemnt, had nonetheless endorsed Minor's interpretation of the Fourteenth in one of her own speeches. She also published the resolutions in the *Revolution*, which she and Anthony still owned in 1869.

The argument that women were included in the Fourteenth Amendment's protections came next to the attention of Victoria Woodhull, a stockbroker on Wall Street. She sent a memorial to the Senate and House of Representatives outlining the argument and asked Congress to declare that women, indeed, had the right to vote. The Judiciary Committee of the House of Representatives invited Woodhull to speak, which she did on January 11, 1871.

Although the Judiciary Committee's report said that nothing in the Fourteenth Amendment entitled women to vote, women around the country refused to give up the idea. In 1871 and 1872, they showed up at the polls. Many women were turned away, but about 150 actually voted. Susan B. Anthony was among the successful voters and she—along with 14 others—was promptly arrested. Since she was a woman, she was unable to testify in her own defense. When she was found guilty and fined $100.00, she vowed never to pay even one cent.

Virginia Minor was one of the women turned away from the polls. She—and her husband, since married women were not allowed to bring legal action on their own—petitioned the courts of St. Louis for damages in the amount of $10,000.00. The case went to the Supreme Court. In 1874, that body rendered its decision: Under the U.S. Constitution, women had no right of suffrage.

As 1876 and the United States' centennial approached, Cady Stanton could not help being upset. The nation was now 100 years old and American women were not yet voting citizens. When she learned that the Declaration of Independence was to be read during an official celebration, she prepared another declaration of her own: the Declaration of Rights for Women. She then asked for permission to deliver the document. "We do not ask to read our declaration," she wrote, "only to present it to the president of the United States, that it may become an historical part of the proceedings."

Permission was refused. Feisty as ever, Cady Stanton began to plan an "overt action" with Anthony and other NWSA members.

On July 4, 1876, Vice-President Thomas Ferry stood in Philadelphia before American citizens and the visiting sovereigns of Europe. The Declaration of Independence was read and loudly cheered. Then Susan B. Anthony and a fellow NWSA member, Matilda Joslyn Gage, walked without invitation to the platform. On behalf of their countrywomen, they presented a "bewildered" Vice-President Ferry with the Declaration of Rights for Women. It contained articles of impeachment against the male government of the United States, and it concluded with an earnest plea: "We ask justice, we ask equality, we ask that all the civil and political rights that belong to citizens of the United States, be guaranteed to us and our daughters forever."

But the justice they so earnestly requested would not be granted soon. Four years later, in July of 1878, the still-disenfranchised women of America celebrated an anniversary of their own: The 30th Anniversary of the Seneca Falls Convention. The celebratory meeting was held in Rochester, New York. No generals, no crowned heads of state attended, but— more gratifying to Elizabeth Cady Stanton—women came or sent letters from all across America and from abroad as well.

Lucretia Mott was present. She was now 86 years old, and this would be her last convention. She seemed to know this and whispered to Cady Stanton: "How thankful I am for these bright young women now ready to fill our soon-to-be vacant places. I want to shake hands with them all before I go, and give them a few words of encouragement."

Elizabeth Cady Stanton spoke of all that had happened since Seneca Falls. Then, at the end of her speech, she too turned to the next generation of women:

> I urge the young women especially to prepare themselves to take up the work so soon to fall from our hands. You have had opportunities for education such as we have not. You hold to-day the vantage-ground we have won by argument. Show now your gratitude to us by making the uttermost of yourselves, and by your earnest, exalted lives secure to those who come after you a higher outlook . . . a larger freedom . . .

The work she talked of passing on was becoming arduous for her. Writing to Libby Miller in 1879 about the commitments that remained before her summer vacation, Cady Stanton lamented: "Two months more containing 61 days still stretch their long length before me. I must pack and unpack my trunk 61 times, pull out the black silk train and don it, curl my hair . . . 61 more times . . . eat 183 more miserable meals . . . [and] avoid making an impression that I am 70, when in reality I feel more like crawling than walking." When she was injured in an omnibus accident and then contracted pneumonia, Cady Stanton decided to retire from the lecture circuit.

At home in Tenafly the November she turned 65, Elizabeth Cady Stanton tried to vote in the 1880 election. Although her ballot was refused, she wrote to two of her children that "I had great fun frightening and muddling these old Dutch inspectors. The whole town is agape with my act."

She also tried to re-establish important relationships. As soon as she recovered from pneumonia, she set off on one more round of travel. Before the end of the decade, she visited her cousin Libby Smith Miller in upstate New York; her sisters Tryphena and Harriet, and then sons Henry and Robert, in New York City; her sister Margaret and son Gerrit in Iowa; her daughter Margaret in Nebraska; and her son Daniel in transit between Nebraska and New York.

Two of her children now lived abroad. Harriot was attending graduate school in England. Theodore, who would write *The Woman Question in Europe*, was living in France. Cady Stanton spent 18 months at a time in Europe with these children.

Elizabeth and Henry did not have a long, settled retirement together. In 1884, just before Henry turned 80, he gave a speech at the Johnstown courthouse. Afterward, Elizabeth wrote with pleasure in her diary that her husband "retains much of his old fire and oratorical power." When he turned 80 on June 27, 1885, he was working as a writer for the New York *Sun*, and his friends and colleagues threw a party at the New York Press Club. Elizabeth, in a letter to Libby Smith Miller, acknowledged Henry's advancing age and added, " . . . I feel my first duty is to make a home for him." Henry's children shared this feeling. The following summer, they gathered in Tenafly. Five grandchildren accompanied them: Florence, born to Daniel and his wife, Fredericka; Nora, born to Harriot and her husband, William Blatch; and Elizabeth, Robert, and Helene, all born to Theodore and his wife, Marguerite Berry. It was, however, the last summer Henry would spend with his family. He died suddenly on January 14, 1887.

Elizabeth was visiting Harriot in Europe and was unable to reach the United States in time for Henry's funeral. She was so devastated that she spent the next month in bed. " . . . when the news comes," she wrote, "the heart and pulses all seem to stand still. We cannot realize that those we have known in life are suddenly withdrawn, to be seen no more on earth. To be with them during their last sickness, to close their eyes, to look upon their lifeless form for the final days, and to go through the sad pageant that follows, helps one, little by little, to realize the change. But when the boundless ocean rolls between you and the lost one, and the startling news comes upon you without preparation, it is a terrible shock to every nerve and feeling, to body and mind alike." Before dying, Henry had mailed his wife a newspaper he knew would interest her; when it arrived she placed the wrapper, addressed to her in his hand, inside her diary. They had been married 46 years.

Henry's death was not the only loss Cady Stanton had to endure during this time. On November 13, 1880, the day after her own 65th birthday, she learned of the death of Lucretia Mott. Cady Stanton had loved and admired Mott for many years. Unable to attend the funeral, she set the day aside for reflection. "This Sunday was with me a sacred memorial day to her," she wrote. "I have vowed again, as I have so many times, that I shall in the future try to imitate her noble example."

Within a few weeks, she, Anthony, and Matilda Joslyn Gage began a project once discussed with Mott: the *History of Woman Suffrage*. It was an incredible undertaking. Cady Stanton planned to document every achievement of women in America, and the history of the organized women's movement as well. When Lucy Stone heard this, she objected. "In regard to the History of the Woman's Rights Movement, I do not think it *can* be written by any one who is alive today . . . when the greatest of all the world movements will have made history . . . *then* it can be written." Cady Stanton thought otherwise: "The United States has not completed its grand experiment of equality," she assured Anthony, " . . . and yet [the historian] Bancroft has been writing our history for forty years."

Volume I was completed in six months. Its 878 pages, dedicated to the memory of Lucretia Mott and 18 other deceased women's rights activists, contained a discussion of "Preceding Causes" that reached all the way back to ancient Egypt; a review of women's work in the newspaper industry throughout the world and beginning in 1702; and then, a careful documentation of the women's rights movement in America, from its beginning at the World Anti-Slavery Convention in London, 1840, to the last National Woman's Rights Convention before the Civil War, in 1860. It also included a chapter on women's place in religious history. There was only one problem: The one publisher willing to accept it insisted that its authors bear part of the expense.

Amelia Willard was still housekeeper in Cady Stanton's home. In the 1850s, she'd donned bloomers. In the 1870s, she'd made it possible for Cady Stanton to travel eight months of every year. "Dear Amelia," Cady Stanton once wrote from Indianapolis, "Take things as easily as you can, and be assured I appreciate your faithful service and all the self-sacrifice you have made for me. My life work, if worth anything to the race, is due in large measure to the leisure your executive ability has secured to me . . ." Now, Amelia Willard donated her life's savings of $3000 and joined other feminists in securing publication of the *History of Woman Suffrage*.

Cady Stanton, Anthony, and Gage were thrilled when the *History* received "splendid notices" in the *Tribune* and the *Sun*.

Elizabeth Cady Stanton and Susan B. Anthony writing the History of Woman Suffrage *(Courtesy of Seneca Falls Historical Society)*

They began Volume II that same summer, in June of 1881. "I am in the toils of another thousand-paged volume," Cady Stanton soon wrote. "My large room with a bay-window is the literary workshop. In the middle is a big library table, and there Susan and I sit . . . laughing, talking, squabbling, day in and day out, buried in illegible manuscripts, old newspapers, and reams of yellow sheets." Gage, busy with family responsibilities, came for a month at a time when she could. Harriot Stanton came from England to help. And Anthony, inheriting $25,000 from a wealthy supporter to be spent "for the advancement of the woman's cause," hired a stenographer to work on the project. Finally, in

1882, Volume II was published. It began with Northern women's contributions during the Civil War and ended in 1875.

Thankfully, it was not until 1884 that Susan B. Anthony once again arrived with boxes containing "masses of unsorted Congressional and suffrage reports, and wholly unsystematized newspaper clippings." Volume III was not completed until 1886. It brought American women's history up to 1885, and included chapters about the history of women in Canada, Great Britain, and Continental Europe. Closing with the personal reminiscences of Elizabeth Cady Stanton, it brought the total output to just under 3,000 pages.

Cady Stanton and Anthony had been in nearly daily contact during this project. Theirs was a relationship that, after 35 years, needed no refurbishing. "Our friendship," Cady Stanton said, "is of too long standing and has too deep roots to be easily shattered. I think we have said worse things to each other, face to face, than we have ever said about each other. Nothing that Susan could say or do could break my friendship with her; and I know nothing could uproot her affection for me."

As 1888 and the 40th Anniversary of Seneca Falls approached, the two friends began to plan something more than a celebration. They began to plan a meeting of an International Council of Women. This idea had first occurred to Cady Stanton during an 1882 trip to Europe. Although she'd gone primarily to visit her children, she'd been welcomed to England and then France as the famous woman she now was. Anthony joined her, and women's rights activists from both countries flocked to their sides. Now these French and English women, and many others, would be invited to the United States.

On March 25, 1888, the first international women's rights convention opened in Washington, D.C. Delegates came from Canada, India, Finland, Denmark, Norway, France, Italy, Ireland, and England. Lucy Stone shared a platform with Cady Stanton and Anthony for the first time in 19 years, and members of both the NWSA and AWSA attended. Other American women represented "Literary Clubs, Art Unions, Temperance Unions, Labor Leagues, Missionary, Peace and Moral Purity [anti-prostitution] Societies, Charitable, Professional, Educational and Industrial Associations." Many of these organizations could not have been imagined 40 years before.

Women from around the world discussed women's progress in various countries. Anthony spoke for the Americans: "From a condition, as many of you can remember, in which no woman thought of earning her bread by any other means than sewing, teaching, cooking or factory work, in these later years the way has been opened to every avenue of industry . . . Men have granted us . . . everything almost but the pivotal right . . . the right to vote."

Cady Stanton, in her turn, preferred to emphasize the commonality of women everywhere. "Whether our feet are compressed in iron shoes, our faces hidden with veils and masks; whether yoked with cows to draw the plow through its furrows, or classed with idiots, lunatics, and criminals in the laws and constitutions of the State, the principle is the same . . . With the spirit forever in bondage, it is the same whether housed in golden cages with every want supplied, or wandering in the dreary deserts of life . . ."

In 1848, at Seneca Falls, 100 Americans had ratified a Declaration of Rights and Sentiments on behalf of women. Now, 40 years later, an international gathering of women unanimously ratified resolutions just as far-reaching:

International Council of Women, 1888 (Courtesy of Seneca Falls Historical Society)

all institutions of learning and of professional instruction, including schools of theology, law and medicine, should . . . be as freely opened to women as to men, and . . .opportunities for industrial training should be as generally and as liberally provided for one sex as the other. The representatives of organized womanhood in this Council will steadily demand that . . . equal wages shall be paid for equal work; and . . . an identical standard of personal purity and morality [shall apply] for men and women.

International women were not the only women united at the end of the 1880s. After the council, negotiations were begun to merge the AWSA and the NWSA. The united National-American Woman Suffrage Association made its debut on February 18, 1890. Elizabeth Cady Stanton was elected president; Susan B. Anthony, vice president; Lucy Stone, chair of the Executive Committee; and Alice Stone Blackwell, the daughter of Lucy Stone, its corresponding secretary.

Although Cady Stanton had regretted the split, she soon became alarmed at a characteristic of the larger, merged organization. Its many younger members had been privileged to grow up in largely reformed circumstances: They had had access to secondary schools and colleges, entered professions in ever-increasing numbers, and were able to own property in many states, even after marriage. They wanted suffrage, Cady Stanton thought, as just one more privilege, and not because it gave them the power to protect every other one of their rights. Worse, many women were beginning to say they should have suffrage because American society would benefit from their use of it. If women voted, they said, public drunkenness would no longer be permitted. Women, they said, were peaceable and would never vote triggerhappy males into office. And orphans, they said, would receive better care if women were among the voters.

Cady Stanton did not doubt that some of these were laudable goals. But she had never argued on behalf of the public benefits that might follow women's enfranchisement. She had argued on behalf of women's inalienable, natural right to liberty. In 1892, at the annual meeting of the National-American Woman Suffrage Association, she very seriously addressed those assembled. The speech was called "The Solitude of Self," and she thought it her best and most important.

"The point I wish plainly to bring before you on this occasion is the individuality of each human soul," she began. " . . . The strongest reason why we ask for woman a voice in the government under which she lives; in the religion she is asked to believe; equality in social life, where she is the chief factor; a place in the trades and professions, where she may earn her bread, is because of her birthright to self-sovereignty; because, as an individual, she must rely on herself . . . it is the height of cruelty to rob the individual of a single natural right . . . To throw obstacles in the way of a complete education is like putting out the eyes; to deny the rights of property is like cutting off the hands . . ."

She continued earnestly, trying to make her audience understand. "The talk of sheltering woman from the fierce storms of life is the sheerest mockery, for they beat on her from every point of the compass, just as they do on man, and with more fatal results, for he has been trained to protect himself, to resist, and to conquer . . . Whatever the theories may be of woman's dependence on man, in the supreme moments of her life, he cannot bear her burdens. Alone she goes to the gates of death to give life to every man that is born into the world; no one can share her fears, no one can mitigate her pangs; and if her sorrow is greater than she can bear, alone she passes beyond the gates into the vast unknown."

Woman's personhood and her claim to all her rights could be found, she stressed, in " . . . those hours of solitude that come alike to all, whether prepared or otherwise . . . a solitude which each and every one of us has always carried with him, more inaccessible than the ice-cold mountains, more profound than the midnight sea; the solitude of self. Our inner being which we call ourself, no eye nor touch of man or angel has ever pierced . . ."

Quietly, she ended her speech. "Such is individual life. Who, I ask you, can take, dare take on himself the rights, the duties, the responsibilities of another human soul?"

Elizabeth Cady Stanton stepped down. President of the National Woman Suffrage Association for many of its 20 years, president of the united National-American Woman Suffrage Association, she now resigned her post. "I am a leader of thought rather than numbers," she had earlier told a friend. "I would rather be a free-lance article . . . than to speak as president of an Association."

8

ETERNAL REALMS: 1893–1902

When Elizabeth Cady Stanton turned 80 years old on November 12, 1895, women threw a party. The Metropolitan Opera Hall was rented. Her well-known name was spelled in a banner made of flowers. Over 6,000 people rose to greet her when she entered the hall, and a chorus of children sang a melody. The Women's Association of Utah sent a ballot box made of polished onyx and silver; a group of Shaker women sent a poem; and the New York City Suffrage League's members presented a loving cup of solid silver. Everywhere Cady Stanton turned, there were flowers, banners, and upturned faces.

Letters and telegrams arrived from around the world. One spoke with particular eloquence: "Every woman who seeks the legal custody of her children; who finds the door of a college or university open to her; who administers a post-office or a public library; who enters upon a career of medicine, law or theology; who teaches school or tills a farm or keeps a shop or rides a bicycle—every such woman owes her liberty largely to yourself and to your earliest and bravest co-workers."

The Seneca Falls Convention had taken place 47 years earlier. Now Cady Stanton had to lean on a cane to address her audience. She could not stand long. She said she accepted the outpouring as belonging, not to her personally, but "to the great idea I represent—the enfranchisement of women."

As the evening drew to a close, the thousands gathered in her honor began gently to sing "Auld Lang Syne." Cady Stanton, "accustomed for half a century to blame rather than praise," was overwhelmed.

She returned that night to an apartment filled with yet more flowers, gifts, letters, telegrams—and one soon-to-be-published book. That book would, she knew, put an end to tributes such as the one she'd just received. It was Volume 1 of *The Woman's Bible*.

Religion was not a new concern to her. As a little girl, she'd shocked her nursemaid by naming God as the source of her childhood troubles. As a child attending a Presbyterian church with an entire pew segregated for its one black member, and as an adult Sunday school teacher whose black students were made to cry, she'd seen cruel hypocrisy on the part of "church members in good standing" and their spiritual leaders. At the World Anti-Slavery Convention in London, it had been the Bible-waving clergy who'd been most against the women and, after the Seneca Falls Convention, they had issued the most searing of the condemnations.

Certainly, these were not her only impressions of religion. Reverend Hossack had kindly taught her Greek. Lucretia Mott and Antoinette Brown had been accepted as ministers in their respective faiths. She herself had sometimes taken her children to church and had composed what she thought was a fitting dinnertime grace: "Heavenly Father and Mother, make us thankful for all the blessings of this life, and make us ever mindful of the patient hands that oft in weariness spread our tables and prepare our daily food. For Humanity's sake, Amen."

But in the years since Seneca Falls, she had come to see the religions dominant in America as obstacles in woman's way. As she explained it, "The Bible teaches that woman brought sin and death into the world, that she precipitated the fall of the race, that she was arraigned before the judgment seat of Heaven, tried, condemned and sentenced. Marriage was for her to be a condition of bondage, maternity a period of suffering and anguish, and in silence and subjection, she was to play the role of a dependent on man's bounty for all her material wants, and for all the information she might desire on the vital questions of the hour, she was commanded to ask her husband at home. Here," Cady Stanton concluded, "is the Bible position of woman briefly summed up."

This biblical position was accepted as "The Word of God," she said, not only by rabbis, ministers, and priests, but "by statesmen in the halls of legislation, [and] by lawyers in the courts . . ." It was "echoed by the press of all civilized nations, and accepted by woman herself." The biblical idea of woman was, she decided, the basis for all discriminatory law: "Creeds, codes, Scriptures, and statutes" alike, defined her as "an inferior being, subject to man." And so, Elizabeth Cady Stanton decided to revise the Bible.

She noted in her introduction that she was not the first person to do this. Men had met many times to revise the Bible, she assured her readers: Each translation into another language, and each modernization within a particular language, had involved a revising committee. (For her own analysis, she used the most recently revised edition, that of 1888.)

She also countered another anticipated charge. "Why," she asked, "is it more ridiculous for woman to protest her present status in the Old and New Testament, in the ordinances and discipline of the church, than in the statutes and constitution of the state? Why is it more ridiculous to arraign ecclesiastics for their false teaching and acts of injustice to women, than members of Congress and the House of Commons? Why is it more audacious to review Moses than Blackstone, the Jewish code of laws, than the English system of jurisprudence?"

Satisfied that the undertaking was not ridiculous, she issued a call for women to join a revising committee. Nineteen American women and five European women agreed to help, but most of the analysis and commentary was, in the end, Elizabeth Cady Stanton's. She herself did "not believe that any man ever saw or talked with God . . . [or] that God . . . told the historians what they say he did about women." Nevertheless, she approached the Bible on its own terms, searching for evidence within the text that clergy had misrepresented the Bible's true position on women.

She contrasted, for example, the two accounts of human creation in the Book of Genesis. Genesis, chapter 1, verses 26 through 28, records the event as follows: "And God said, Let us make man in our image, and after our likeness: and let them have dominion . . . So God created man in his *own* image, in the image of God created he him; male and female created he them. And God blessed them, and God said unto them, Be fruitful, and multiply . . . and have dominion over the fish of the sea, and over the fowl of the air, and over every living thing that moveth upon the earth." According to this version, God, using the plural possessive pronoun, "our," is plural; and since the man created "in our image" is "male and female," Cady

Stanton says "we have in these texts a declaration of the existence of the feminine element in the Godhead, equal in power and glory with the masculine. The Heavenly Mother and Father!" And if woman and man were simultaneously created, each in the respective image of a "Mother and Father" God, how, she asks, "is it possible to make woman an afterthought?" Concluding this section of her analysis, she points out that "equal dominion is given to woman over every living thing, but not one word is said giving man dominion over woman."

Genesis, chapter 2, verses 21–25, tells a different story, a story usually used to explain women's second place status: the creation of Eve from one of Adam's ribs. If Eve's creation, or birth, "of the man," placed her in a subordinate position, Cady Stanton argued, then the same principle could be used to reach a different conclusion today. All present-day men had been born of human mothers, "of the woman," Cady Stanton pointed out. Should this make men's "place . . . one of subjection?" If not, she thought, then Eve's place had also been incorrectly assigned, and "the equal position declared in the first account must prove more satisfactory to both sexes; created alike in the image of God—The Heavenly Mother and Father."

Cady Stanton next turned her attention to Genesis, chapter 3, verses 1–24: the account of Eve's temptation by the serpent. "And the woman said unto the serpent . . . the fruit of the tree which *is* in the midst of the garden, God hath said Ye shall not eat of it . . . lest ye die. And the serpent said unto the woman, Ye shall not surely die; For God doth know that in the day ye eat thereof then your eyes shall be opened, and ye shall be as gods, knowing good and evil. And when the woman saw that the tree *was* . . . to be desired to make *one* wise, she took of the fruit thereof, and did eat and gave also unto her husband with her; and he did eat. And the eyes of them both were opened . . . Unto the woman he [God] said, I will greatly multiply thy sorrow and thy conception; in sorrow thou shall bring forth children; and thy desire *shall be* to thy husband, and he shall rule over thee. And unto Adam he said, Because thou hast hearkened unto the voice of thy wife, and hast eaten of the tree cursed *is* the ground for thy sake . . . And the Lord God said, Behold the man *is* become as one of us, to know good and evil; and now, . . . the Lord God sent him forth from the garden of Eden, to till the ground from whence he was taken."

Eve was, as far as Cady Stanton was concerned, a heroine. Before this, life in the garden had been a timeless, challenge-less non-event, spent "picking flowers and talking with Adam, [which] did not satisfy." When reading this account, Cady Stanton said, "the unprejudiced reader must be impressed with the courage, the dignity, and the lofty ambition of the woman. The tempter . . . did not try to tempt her . . . by brilliant jewels, rich dresses, worldly luxuries or pleasures, but with the promise of knowledge, with the wisdom of the Gods"—which, according to the account, she does in fact attain.

So far as the curse upon woman, Cady Stanton decided it had been "inserted in an unfriendly spirit to justify her degradation and subjection to man." Pregnancy and childbirth were, despite the "supposed curse" of God, perfectly wonderful events for many women. Even Sarah, Abraham's wife, "forgot that maternity was intended as a curse on all Eve's daughters." As one proof, Cady Stanton pointed out that "Sarah is represented through several chapters as laughing, even in the presence of angels, not only in anticipation of the event [of Isaac's birth], but in its realization."

Lillie Deveraux Blake, author, suffragist, and great-great-granddaughter of Jonathan Edwards, the Puritan preacher, also examined this account. " . . . We are amazed that upon such a story men have built up a theory of their superiority!"

Clara Bewick Colby, president for 13 years of the Nebraska Woman Suffrage Association and editor of the *Woman's Tribune*, turned her attention to the curse upon Adam and his male descendants. "For Adam, not Eve," she wrote, "the earth was to bring forth the thorn and the thistle, and he was to eat his bread by the sweat of his brow. Yet I never heard a sermon on the sin of uprooting weeds, or letting Eve, as she does, help him to bear his burden. It is when she tries to lighten her load that the world is afraid of sacrilege and the overthrow of nature."

Volume 1 of *The Woman's Bible*, covering the Old Testament Books of Genesis, Exodus, Leviticus, Numbers, and Deuteronomy, was published in 1895, just two weeks after Cady Stanton's 80th birthday party. She expected the book to bring two kinds of criticism. The first would come, she thought, from those who considered the Bible a relic from the past. These people, and especially women's rights activists seeking concrete change, would believe she had wasted her time. Susan B. Anthony certainly felt that way. As she wrote to Cady Stanton, "Barbarism does not grow out of ancient Jewish Bibles—but out of our own sordid meanness!! . . . stop hitting poor old St. Paul—and give your heaviest raps on the head of every . . . man or woman—who does injustice to a human being—for the crime of color or sex! . . . I do wish you could center your big brain on the crimes we, ourselves, as a people, are responsible for—to charge *our* offenses to false books or false interpretations—is but a way of seeking a *refuge of lies.*"

Others, regarding the Bible as a sacred, divinely inspired work, would, she expected, be offended on other grounds. She was correct.

The Woman's Bible had seven printings in just six months and was published in England, but it became a scandal as well as a best-seller. Cady Stanton was branded a heretic. One clergyman went so far as to declare that *The Woman's Bible* was "the work of women, and the devil." Cady Stanton was not upset and issued a breezy response. "This is a grave mistake. His Satanic Majesty was not invited to join the Revising Committee, which consists of women alone. Moreover, he has been so busy of late years attending Synods, General Assemblies and Conferences, to prevent the recognition of women delegates, that he has had no time . . ." She was genuinely glad to cause such a ruckus. As she wrote to Antoinette Blackwell, "We have had hearings before Congress for 18 years steadily, good reports, good votes but no action." In contrast, this was a productive "attack on some new quarter of the enemies' domain. Our politicians are calm and complacent under our fire but the clergy jump round . . . like parched peas on a hot shovel."

She was not so delighted by the criticism of the National American Woman Suffrage Association. Its younger members, as she had realized when she resigned the presidency, were more conservative than she. The women of this younger generation were not interested in radical re-analysis of society's foundations. They worked to make the demand for women suffrage seem respectable and nonthreatening. When *The Woman's Bible* was published, they were livid. At its January 1896 meeting, a resolution repudiating "the so-called 'Woman's Bible'" was introduced.

Susan B. Anthony (photo by Grace Woodworth; Courtesy of Seneca Falls Historical Society)

Susan B. Anthony was president of NWSA at the time, and she was acting as chairperson at this meeting. As soon as the resolution was introduced, she stepped down from the chair to defend Elizabeth Cady Stanton, who was not present.

"The one distinct feature of our Association has been the right of individual opinion for every member," she began. " . . . What you should do is to say to outsiders that a Christian has neither more nor less rights in our Association than an atheist. When our platform becomes too narrow for people of all creeds and of no creed, I myself shall not stand upon it. Many things have been said and done by our orthodox friends that I have felt to be extremely harmful to our cause; but I should no more consent to a resolution denouncing them than I shall consent to this. Who is to draw the line? Who can tell now whether Mrs. Stanton's commentaries may not prove a great help to woman's emancipation from old superstitions that have barred her way? Lucretia

Mott at first thought Mrs. Stanton had injured the cause of all woman's other rights by insisting upon the demand for suffrage, but she had sense enough not to bring in a resolution against it. In 1860, when Mrs. Stanton made a speech before the New York state legislature in favor of a bill making drunkenness a cause for divorce, there was a general cry among the friends that she had killed the woman's cause. I shall be pained beyond expression if the delegates here are so narrow and illiberal as to adopt this resolution . . . I pray you, vote for religious liberty, without censorship or inquisition. This resolution, adopted, will be a vote of censure upon a woman who is without peer in intellectual and statesmanlike ability; one who has stood for half a century the acknowledged leader of pro-

Elizabeth Cady Stanton (photo by Grace Woodworth; Courtesy of Seneca Falls Historical Society)

gressive thought and demand in regard to all matters pertaining to the absolute freedom of women."

Despite Anthony's plea, the resolution was adopted. Cady Stanton was deeply hurt by this, and by Anthony's refusal to resign as NWSA's president in protest. Nonetheless, she began work on Volume II of *The Woman's Bible*. Published in 1898, it began with the Old Testament Book of Joshua and ended with the New Testament Book of Revelation. Anthony's speech in her defense was included in the appendix—as was NWSA's resolution. It was one of her last acts of protest.

In the beginning of the following year, Harriot took her mother to a doctor. He diagnosed cataracts. When the two women were alone again, in their carriage, Harriot took her mother's hand. Cady Stanton whispered, as if to herself: "And both eyes." She never again spoke of her impending blindness to her children. In her diary though, she mourned the loss of her sight: "my eyes grow dimmer from day to day . . . I have written Susan not to lay out any more work for me . . ."

Nevertheless, she continued to work for suffrage until the very end of her life. On October 25, 1902, she dictated a letter to President Theodore Roosevelt:

> In the beginning of our nation, the fathers declared that 'no just government can be founded without the consent of the governed,' and that 'taxation without representation is tyranny.' Both of these grand declarations are denied in the present position of women, who constitutes one-half of the people. If 'political power inheres in the people'—and women are surely people—then there is crying need for an amendment to the National Constitution, making these fundamental principles verities . . .
>
> Abraham Lincoln immortalized himself by the emancipation of four million Southern slaves. Speaking for my suffrage coadjutors, we now desire that you, Mr. President, who are already celebrated for so many honorable deeds and worthy utterances, immortalize yourself by bringing about the complete emancipation of thirty-six million women.
>
> With best wishes for your continued honorable career and re-election as President of the United States . . .

It was the last of her letters. On October 26, 1902, just a few weeks short of her 87th birthday, Elizabeth Cady Stanton died.

9

EPILOGUE

On the eve of World War I, Harriot Stanton Blatch faced a dilemma. Members of the Woman's party, to which she belonged, had begun picketing the White House on January 10, 1917, demanding suffrage. They received sympathetic words from some passersby and disparagement from others. They were not arrested: In the United States, there was no law against picketing.

Blatch knew there could be trouble, though, if the United States were at war and the women continued protesting. But after much hard thought, she issued her opinion: "The suffragists of Civil War days [gave up] their campaign to work for their country, expecting to be enfranchised for all their good services, but when the war was over, they heard on all sides, 'This is the Negro's hour.' They were told they must wait, their turn would come next. My mother and Miss Anthony led the small rebel group who were not willing to wait. But women did not rally behind them. They stepped aside for the Negro. Now in 1917 women [are] still waiting." When the United States entered the war, the Woman's party pickets remained outside the White House gates.

Carrie Chapman Catt, who was the National American Woman Suffrage Association's president at this time, did not approve of the Woman's party's tactics. NAWSA had continued to pursue both the state-by-state and the federal route to suffrage, with some success, at least on the state level. At the end of 1916, women could vote in eight states: Wyoming, Utah, Colorado, Idaho, Kansas, Oregon, Montana, and Nevada. Catt had also worked hard to build a rapport with President Wilson, and to enlist his support for a women's suffrage amendment to the United States Constitution. The Woman's party, under leaders Alice Paul and Lucy Burns, and with members as uncompromising as Harriot Stanton Blatch, endangered the respectable image Catt sought for the cause.

But Catt, too, refused to suspend the women's movement during World War I. She motivated her members to help in the war effort, and women responded in the by now familiar and even expected ways. They served at the front as nurses, filled the "male" jobs that soldiers left behind, and made the weapons. (Physical exams for soldiers now prevented women from enlisting in disguise.) The National American Woman Suffrage Association even had its own hospital in Europe, the Overseas Hospital. But not one women's rights action was canceled this time, and suffrage parades—by now a customary sight in city streets—attracted thousands. When Red Cross and other female war volunteers joined the New York City parade on October 27, 1918, both NAWSA and Woman's party leaders hoped their countrymen noticed.

The Woman's party leaders knew that the White House picketers had been noticed. On June 22, 1819, the first of these women had been arrested and charged with the only possible charge: obstructing traffic on a sidewalk. Found guilty of this charge, Alice Paul and 96 other suffragists served sentences of up to six months. In jail, they were physically abused, put into solitary confinement and, when they refused to eat, force-fed. Several of the women had to be taken by ambulance to their trials. The women believed they were jailed for their political beliefs. On scraps of paper, they composed a document claiming political prisoner status, and they managed to pass it from woman to woman for signing. It was the first time that a United States citizen had made such a claim. Eventually, the District of Columbia Court of Appeals found each of the arrests and imprisonments "invalid."

In the meantime, NAWSA had continued to work for state suffrage; in 1917, six more states extended suffrage to women. (One, Ohio, also rescinded it before the year was out, making the need for a federal amendment all the more obvious to the suffragists.) Carrie Chapman Catt had also continued to urge President Wilson to intervene directly with the Congress. On September 30, 1918, he did so. Taking the rare step of addressing the Senate in person to ask for a specific vote, he said:

We have made partners of the women in this war; shall we admit them only to a partnership of suffering and sacrifice and toil and not to a partnership of privilege and right? This war could not have been fought, either by the other nations engaged or by America, if it had not been for the services of women—services rendered in every sphere— not merely in the fields of effort in which we have been accustomed to see them work, but wherever men have worked, and upon the very skirts and edges of the battle itself . . . I tell you plainly, that this measure which I urge upon you is vital to the winning of the war . . . and not to the winning of the war only. It is vital to the right solution of the great problems which we must settle, and settle immediately, when the war is over.

The measure—to pass a federal woman suffrage amendment and send it to the states for ratification—failed by only two votes in 1918. The following year, on May 21, 1919, the House of Representatives passed the Nineteenth Amendment. On June 4, 1919, the Senate passed it as well, and sent it to the states for ratification.

The Nineteenth Amendment was adopted on August 26, 1920.

FURTHER READING

The published primary sources to consult for additional information about Elizabeth Cady Stanton are: her autobiography, *80 Years and More: Reminiscences 1815–1897* (1898; rpt. New York: Schocken Books, 1971), *The Woman's Bible* (1895; rpt. Salem, N.H.: Ayer Company, Publishers, Inc., 1988), *Elizabeth Cady Stanton: As Revealed in Her Letters, Diary and Reminiscences*, Theodore Stanton and Harriot Stanton Blatch, eds. (2 vols., 1922; rpt., New York: Arno and The New York Times, 1969) and the *History of Woman Suffrage*, Elizabeth Cady Stanton, Susan B. Anthony et al., eds. (6 vols., 1881–1922; rpt., Salem, N.H.: Ayer Company, Publishers, Inc., 1985). See also *Elizabeth Cady Stanton / Susan B. Anthony: Correspondence, Writings, Speeches,* Ellen Carol DuBois, ed. (New York: Schocken Books, 1981).

Unpublished primary sources include the Library of Congress' collection of her letters, of which the New York Public Library has a microfilm copy, and the collection at the Seneca Falls Historical Society Library.

Two other biographies of Elizabeth Cady Stanton are *Elizabeth Cady Stanton: A Radical for Women's Rights*, by Lois Banner (Boston: Little, Brown & Co., 1980); and *In Her Own Right: The Life of Elizabeth Cady Stanton*, by Elisabeth Griffith (New York: Oxford University Press, 1984).

For information about other people in this book, see *Susan B. Anthony: A Biography of a Singular Feminist*, by Kathleen Barry (New York: New York University Press, 1988); *The Life and Work of Susan B. Anthony,* Ida Husted Harper (3 vols., 1891; rpt, Salem, NH: Ayer Company, Publishers, Inc., 1983); *Random Recollections*, 3d ed., by Henry B. Stanton (New York: Harper & Bros., 1887); *Valiant Friend: The Life of Lucretia Mott* (New York: Walker and Company, 1980); *Slavery and "The Woman Question": Lucretia Mott's Diary on Her Visit to Great*

Britain to Attend the World's Anti-Slavery Convention of 1840, Frederick B. Tolles, ed. (Haverford: Friends' Historical Association, Supplement No. 23 to *The Journal of the Friends Historical Society*, 1952); Mary Grew's Diary, 1840 (Woodbridge, Conn.: Research Publications, 1983. Microfilm); "Life and Work in Middlebury, Vermont, of Emma Willard," an address read at Rutland, Vermont, before the Congressional Club, Sept. 26, 1893, by Ezra Brainerd (printed New York: Evening Post Job Printing House [n.d.]); *Emma Willard: Daughter of Democracy*, by Alma Lutz (Boston: 1929); *Emma Willard and Her Pupils: or, Fifty Years of Troy Female Seminary: 1822–1872*, by Mrs. Russell Sage et al. (1898); *Gerrit Smith: Philanthropist and Reformer*, by Ralph Volney Harlow (1939; rpt., New York: Russell & Russell, 1972); *Narrative of the Life of Frederick Douglass, an American Slave*, by Frederick Douglass (1845; rpt., New York: Anchor Books, 1989); *Frederick Douglass on Women's Rights*, Philip S. Foner, ed. (Westport: Greenwood Press, 1976); *Frederick Douglass and the Fight for Freedom* by Douglass T. Miller (New York: Facts On File, Inc., 1988); *We Are Your Sisters: Black Women in the Nineteenth Century*, Dorothy Sterling, ed. (New York: W. W. Norton & Company, 1984); *Loving Warriors: Selected Letters of Lucy Stone and Henry B. Blackwell, 1853 to 1893*, Leslie Wheeler, ed. (New York: The Dial Press, 1981); *Friends and Sisters: Letters between Lucy Stone and Antoinette Brown Blackwell, 1846–93*, Carol Lasser and Marlene Deahl Merrill, eds. (Urbana: University of Chicago Press, 1897); and *Challenging Years: The Memoirs of Harriot Stanton Blatch*, by Harriot Stanton Blatch and Alma Lutz (New York: G.P. Putnam's Sons, 1940). *Notable American Women: A Biographical Dictionary*, Edward T. James, Janet Wilson James and Paul S. Boyer, eds. (3 vols.; Cambridge: The Belnap Press of Harvard University Press, 1971), is also a wonderful source of information.

Two surveys of the woman suffrage movement are *Century of Struggle: The Women's Rights Movement in the United States*, by Eleanor Flexner (Cambridge: Harvard University Press, 1975) and *Women's Suffrage in America: An Eyewitness History*, Elizabeth Frost and Kathryn Cullen-DuPont, eds. (New York: Facts On File) (forthcoming)). For a closer examination of housework in 19th-century America, see *Never Done: A History of American Housework*, by Susan Strasser (New York: Pantheon Books, 1982) and *The American Frugal Housewife*, by Lydia Maria Child

(1833, rpt. Boston: Applewood Books [n.d.]). *For Her Own Good: 150 Years of the Experts' Advice to Women*, by Barbara Ehrenreich and Deidre English (New York: Doubleday, 1989) examines the intertwined issues of housework, medical and psychiatric thought concerning women, and women's clothing as a health hazard.

To learn more about women's part in the Civil War, see "What Women Did for the War, and What the War Did for Women, a Memorial Day Address Delivered Before the Soldier's Club at Wellesley, Massachusetts, May 30, 1894," by Josiah H. Benton, Jr. (Boston, 1894); *Mary Chestnut's Civil War*, C. Vann Woodward, ed. (New Haven: Yale University Press, 1981); *Our Army Nurses: Interesting Sketches, Addresses, And Photographs Of nearly One Hundred of the Noble Women who Served in Hospitals and on Battlefields during Our Civil War*, Mary A. Gardner Holland, ed. (Boston: B. Wilkins & Co., 1895); *My Story of the War: A Woman's Narrative of Four Years Personal Experience As Nurse in The Union Army, And In Relief Work At Home, In Hospitals, Camps And At The Front, During the War Of The Rebellion*, by Mary A. Livermore (1887; rpt., Williamstown, Mass.: Corner Publishers, 1978); *Women in the War; Their Heroism and Self-Sacrifice,* by Frank Moore (Hartford, Conn.: S. S. Scranton & Company, 1866); *Battle Cry of Freedom: The Civil War Era*, by James McPherson (New York: Oxford University Press, 1988); and *Harper's Pictoral History of the Civil War*, Alfred H. Guernsey and Henry M. Alden, eds. (New York: Fairfax Press, 1866).

To learn more about the last phase of the women's suffrage movement, see *Woman Suffrage and Politics*, by Carrie Chapman Catt and Nettie Rogers Shuler (New York: Charles Scribner's Sons, 1923); "The Winning Policy," by Carrie Chapman Catt (New York: National American Woman Suffrage Association, 1916); The Carrie Chapman Catt Papers, Manuscript and Archives Division, New York Public Library; *The Ideas of the Woman Suffrage Movement, 1880–1920*, by Aileen S. Kraditor (New York: W. W. Norton & Company, 1981); and *Jailed for Freedom*, by Doris Stevens (New York: Boni and Liveright Publishers, 1920). Harriot Stanton Blatch's *Memoir*, mentioned above, is also a good source of information about this period.

Recent feminist works regarding women and religion include *When God Was a Woman*, by Merlin Stone (New York: Harcourt Brace Jovanovich, 1976) *Beyond God the Father: Toward a Philosophy of Women's Liberation*, by Mary Daly (Boston: Beacon Press, 1973); and *Eunuchs for the Kingdom of Heaven: The Catholic Church and Sexuality*, by Uta Ranke-Heinemann (New York: Doubleday, 1990).

To learn more about London and its female residents at the time of the World Anti-Slavery Convention, see *A History of London* by Robert Gray (London: Hutchinson & Co., 1978); *London Labour and the London Poor*, by Henry Mayhew (4 vols., 1852–1865; abridged, New York: Viking Penguin, 1985); and *Women's Work in Nineteenth-Century London: A Study of the Years 1820–50*, by Sally Alexander (London: The Journeyman Press, 1983).

For information about New York City and State, see *New York: State and City*, by David Maldwyn Ellis (Ithaca: Cornell University Press, 1979); *The Epic of New York City: A Narrative History*, by Edward Robb Ellis (New York: Old Town Books, 1966); *A History of Seneca Falls, New York, 1779–1862*, by Henry Stowell (reprint, Seneca Falls Historical Society, 1875); and *A Geographical History of the State of New York: Embracing its History, Government, Physical Features, Climate, Geology, Mineralogy, Botany, Zoology, Education, Internal Improvements, etc., with separate Maps of Each County, the Whole Forming a Complete History of the State*, by J. H. Mather and L. P. Brocker (Utica: H.H. Hawley & Co., 1848).

To find out about the ships that sailed between New York and London, see *Queens of the Western Ocean: The Story of America's Mail and Passenger Sailing Lines*, by Carl C. Cutler (Annapolis: United States Naval Institute, 1961) and *The Seafarers: The Atlantic Crossing*, by Melvin Maddocks and the Time Life Editors (Alexandria, Va.: Time-Life Books, 1981).

An excellent collection of documents central to American history is *Soul of America: Documenting Our Past, 1492–1974*, Robert C. Baron, ed. (Golden, Colorado: Fulcrum, Inc., 1989).

Finally, a suggestion for a place to visit: Seneca Falls is home not only to the Seneca Falls Historical Society but to the Women's Rights National Historical Park, which has carefully restored Elizabeth Cady Stanton's Seneca Falls home. The Park Service also maintains a very informative visitor center and has commissioned a replacement of the Wesleyan Chapel, which was torn down long ago; in the meantime, a bronze plaque marks the site. Every summer, the town celebrates the anniversary of the Seneca Falls Convention with a reenactment of the convention, parades, a country fair beside the canal (with music from morning until midnight), and lectures on women's history topics. The Women's Hall of Fame is also located in Seneca Falls.

INDEX

Italic numbers indicate illustrations

others, 61, 66, 71, 76–77, 84–85, 99
Women's surnames, 3, 48–49, 74, 80
Woodhull, Victoria, 95
Woodbridge, William Channing, 33
Worcester Convention, 61–62
World Anti-Slavery Convention, London, 2, 4–5, 8, 11–14, 41, 48, 54, 55, 71, 99

World War I, 115–117
Wright, Martha Coffin, 55, 59, 72, 76–77, 80, 83
Wyoming, women enfranchised, 94

Y

Yost, Marie, 21